Daily Devotion For New Dads

Guidance and Inspiration for the First Year of Fatherhood

Tanya F. Toms

All rights reserved.
No part of this publication may be reproduced, distributed, or transmitted in any form or by any means, including photocopying, recording, or other electronic or mechanical methods, without the prior written permission of the publisher, except in the case of brief quotations embodied in critical reviews and certain other noncommercial uses permitted by copyright law.
Copyright © Tanya F. Toms

TABLE OF CONTENTS

INTRODUCTION.. 3
Welcome to Fatherhood.. 6

Chapter 1: Embracing Fatherhood.................................. 9

A New Beginning... 12
Bonding with Your Baby.. 18
Emotions of Fatherhood..24
Supporting Your Partner... 30
Establishing Routines...38

Chapter 2: Navigating Challenges................................ 46

Sleepless Nights.. 57
Balancing Work and Family....................................... 67
Dealing with Uncertainty.. 78
Patience in Parenthood..88
Coping with Stress.. 98

Chapter 3: Building Strong Connections......................... 108

Playtime with Your Baby.. 117
Creating Family Traditions..................................... 126

Communication with Your Partner............................... 133
Grandparents and Extended Family.............................141
Celebrating Milestones... 151

Chapter 4: Self-Care for Dads.......................................164

Finding Time for Yourself...172
Staying Healthy and Fit.. 181
Mental Well-being...190
Hobbies and Personal Time.. 199
Seeking Support..206

Chapter 5: Looking Ahead...214

Reflections on the First Year...222
Planning for the Future... 231
Embracing Fatherhood Beyond Year One..................... 239
Lessons Learned..247

CONCLUSION...256

INTRODUCTION

Let's start with the larger picture. Fatherhood is a crazy trip, full of shocks, sleepless nights, and heart-melting moments that make it all worthwhile. This book? It's like a daily friend, a pal in the trenches with you, delivering nuggets of knowledge, a dash of inspiration, and a sprinkling of consolation.

Now, why daily devotion? Well, life as a new dad may be a whirlwind. Diapers, feedings, and the lovely chaos of a tiny one may make the days blend together. That's where daily devotion comes in. It's not about adding another item to your to-do list; it's about taking a minute for yourself among the lovely chaos.

In these pages, you'll discover something special—verses from the Good Book, the Bible. Now, you could be thinking, "I'm not particularly religious." That's completely fine. Consider these poems as timeless nuggets of counsel, like the shared knowledge of generations before us. They're here to give comfort, direction, and a bit of perspective.

Take, for instance, Psalm 139:13-14:

*"For you fashioned my internal parts; you knitted me together in my mother's womb.
I praise you, because I am fearfully and wonderfully made.
Wonderful are your works; my soul understands it very well."*

This passage relates to the wonderful design of life, the careful making of each small one. It's a reminder that your path into parenthood is part of a big plan, a masterpiece in the making.

This one touches home for many new parents. It's a reminder to take things one day at a time, not to get weighed down by what tomorrow could bring. Embrace each day, each moment, and find serenity in the present.

As you flip through these pages day by day, think of it as a tiny break, a stop button in the middle of parental turmoil. Some days, you may find solace in the words; other days, a little of challenge or encouragement. It's your time, your daily routine in this magnificent experience called parenthood.

So here's to you, new dad. Here's to the late nights and early mornings, to the laughter and the tears. May these daily devotions be a modest beacon of light on your path, a time of thought and connection. You've got this!

===

Welcome to Fatherhood

===

Becoming a parent is a little like going off on a huge journey, equipped with love, a diaper bag, and an abundance of hope. You're going to see personally the wonder of a new life, a small human who will look up to you with those inquiring eyes, and who will fill your days with laughter, tears, and the sweetest embraces.

As you stand on the verge of parenting, understand this: you're not alone. Millions of parents before you have made this leap, each with their own tale to share. And now, you're contributing your chapter to the big narrative of motherhood.

This is more than simply a position; it's a calling, a chance to mold and be shaped by a new existence. The sleepless nights and the constant rocking of a fussy newborn may seem frightening, but believe me, the pleasure that fills your heart when you see your tiny one smile or hear them say the loveliest babbling makes it all worthwhile.

Let's take a minute to meditate on the wisdom provided in the Bible. Ecclesiastes 3:1 informs us:

"To everything, there is a season and a time to every purpose under heaven."

In your journey as a parent, remember that there's a season for everything. A time for those restless nights and a time for the heart-melting moments. Embrace each moment as part of a meaningful path, and know that you're prepared for any season that comes your way.

Now, let's speak about love. Oh, the love you're going to feel is beyond words. It's a love that develops, evolves, and becomes a force that motivates you to be the greatest parent you can be. 1 Corinthians 16:14 encourages us:

"Let all that you do be done in love."

As you change diapers, sing lullabies, and handle the obstacles of parenthood, do it all with love. It's the secret component that converts ordinary events into amazing memories.

And when the journey becomes rough, when you doubt your capacity to be the parent your young one needs, look to Philippians 4:13:

"I can do all things through him who strengthens me."

You've got a wellspring of power inside you, a strength that comes not only from your own skills but from a heavenly source. Lean on it, particularly when the path seems a little daunting.

So, my fellow dad, welcome to this great trip. It won't always be easy, but it will always be worth it. Your love, your presence, and your commitment are treasures that your young one will remember forever. Here's to you and the incredible path of parenting!

Chapter 1: Embracing Fatherhood

Imagine standing at the entrance of a thrilling roller coaster, the sort that takes unexpected twists and turns, makes your heart beat, and leaves you with a combination of exhilaration and anxiety. Well, my buddy, that's a little like stepping into the shoes of a parent.

To "embrace" parenthood is to gladly accept it, arms wide open, ready for the highs, the lows, and all the magnificent loops in between. It's not only about embracing the part; it's about enveloping oneself in the experience, appreciating every minute, and finding delight in the unexpected.

Now, let's add a little of old knowledge into our discourse. Proverbs 3:5-6 lays the scenario beautifully:

"Trust in the Lord with all your heart, and do not lean on your own understanding. In all your ways acknowledge him, and he will make straight paths."

As you begin on this trip, know that there's a guiding power beyond your understanding. Fatherhood may not always make perfect sense, but have trust that the road you're on is intentional and uniquely yours.

Speaking of individuality, let's speak about your kid. Your tiny one is a masterpiece in the making, made with care and purpose. Psalm 139:13-14 conveys this thought beautifully:

"For you formed my inward parts; you knitted me together in my mother's womb. I praise you, for I am fearfully and wonderfully made."

Your kid is a miracle, fearfully and beautifully formed. Embrace the uniqueness that each day provides, rejoicing in the discovery of the amazing creature in your care.

Now, let's go into the essence of "embracing." It's about love—boundless, unconditional love. 1 Corinthians 16:14 nudges us gently:

"Let all that you do be done in love."

Love becomes the glue that links your trip. From the quiet times of comforting a weeping newborn to the exuberant celebrations of first steps, let love be your guide. It's in the sweet whispers of bedtime tales and the reassuring hugs amid storms.

And while you accept this responsibility, remember that parenthood isn't a solitary effort; it's a dance, a relationship. Ecclesiastes 4:9-10 clearly shows this:

"Two are better than one because they have a good reward for their toil. For if they fall, one will lift up his fellow. But woe to him who is alone when he falls and has not another to lift him up!"

Lean on your companion, share the weight, and enjoy the wins together. Embracing parenthood is about making relationships, developing a support system, and building a family that stands strong through the journey's ups and downs.

Now, let's touch on patience. Oh, the virtue of patience, a jewel in the fabric of parenting. Galatians 6:9 gives a pleasant reminder:

"And let us not grow weary of doing good, for in due season we will reap if we do not give up."

There will be periods of exhaustion, restless nights, and problems that seem insurmountable. But stick in there, because the pleasures of parenting reveal in due season.

Be present in each season of your child's life—be it the wonderful seasons of laughter and play or the quieter seasons of contemplation and development. Embrace the ephemeral moments, because they build the lovely tale of your family.

Now, let's speak about legacy. Your responsibility as a parent isn't only about the moment; it's about the permanent influence you leave. Proverbs 22:6 gives everlasting wisdom:

"Train up a child in the way he should go; even when he is old, he will not depart from it."

Your direction, morals, and love become the compass for your child's path. Embrace the responsibility of establishing a legacy that transcends beyond your years.

===

A New Beginning
===

Becoming a parent is, in many ways, a fresh beginning for both you and your kid. It's a trip that will transform your thoughts, priorities, and, most significantly, your heart. Just as the dawn of each day provides new chances, the birth of your little one heralds a fresh start, a chance to accept the deep duty and privilege of parenthood.

The Miracle of Life

watching the birth of your kid is an awe-inspiring event, similar to watching a miracle unfold before your eyes. The tenderness of a baby, the first scream that fills the room, and the overpowering sensation of responsibility - these moments sear themselves into your mind, marking the beginning of a unique and irreplaceable link.

A Father's Love

As you hold your infant in your arms, you'll experience a love like no other. It's a love that defies words, a love so deep and unconditional that it resembles the divine love talked about in the Bible. In 1 Corinthians 13:4-7 (NIV), we find a beautiful description of love that resonates with the love a father has for his child: "Love is patient, love is kind. It does not envy, it does not boast, it is not proud. It does not dishonor others, it is not self-seeking, it is not easily angered, it keeps no record of wrongs. Love does not delight in evil but rejoices with the truth. It always protects, always trusts, always hopes, always perseveres."

Responsibility and Sacrifice

With the advent of your kid, a new set of obligations accompanies the delight of parenthood. It's a call to selflessness and sacrifice, values reflected in the teachings of Jesus. In Mark 10:45 (NIV), Jesus says, "For even the Son of Man did not come to be served, but to serve, and to give his life as a ransom for many." Embracing your position as a father includes a commitment to serve, sacrifice, and give of yourself for the well-being and happiness of your kid.

Learning and Growing Together

Just as your kid goes on a voyage of discovery, you, too, will embark on a path of learning and development. The Bible encourages a childlike faith in Matthew 18:3 (NIV): "Truly I tell you, unless you change and become like little children, you will never enter the kingdom of heaven." As you navigate the challenges of parenthood, approach them with a humble and teachable heart, much like the openness and curiosity of a child.

Nurturing & Guidance

Your responsibility as a father entails not simply providing for your child's bodily necessities but also fostering their emotional, spiritual, and mental well-being. Proverbs 22:6 (NIV) underscores the significance of guiding your kid: "Start children off on the way they should go, and even when they are old, they will not turn from it." Your influence and direction determine the path your child pursues, shaping their character and values.

Patience in the Journey

Parenthood is a journey defined by milestones, failures, and the ordinary moments that weave the fabric of family life. It demands patience, a virtue emphasised in James 1:4 (NIV): "Let perseverance finish its work so that you may be mature and complete, not lacking anything." Just as a toddler learns to walk with patience and practice, so too will you develop as a father through the struggles and victories of each day.

Building Memories

"A New Beginning" is not only about the present but also about the legacy you establish for your kid. Ecclesiastes 3:1 (NIV) tells us, "There is a time for everything, and a season for every activity under the heavens." Each minute you spend with your kid adds to the tapestry of memories that will define their concept of love, family, and life.

Strength in Vulnerability

In your journey as a parent, embrace vulnerability. It takes guts to recognise when you don't have all the answers and to seek assistance when required. Proverbs 3:5-6 (NIV) emphasises faith and dependence on God: "Trust in the Lord with all your heart and lean not on your own understanding; in all your ways submit to him, and he will make your paths straight." As a parent, rely in the supernatural wisdom that exceeds human understanding.

Joy in the Ordinary

Find delight in the regular moments. It's tempting to concentrate on spectacular gestures, but frequently, the most lasting bonds are created in the simplicity of shared laughter, bedtime tales, and family dinners. Philippians 4:4 (NIV) supports an attitude of joy: "Rejoice in the Lord always. I will say it again: Rejoice!" Let this joy permeate your household and your connection with your kid.

A Legacy of Love

As you start on this fresh beginning, realise that your effect reaches beyond the immediate. Psalm 103:17-18 (NIV) speaks of the lasting impact of God's love: "But from everlasting to everlasting the Lord's love is with those who fear him, and his righteousness with their children's children — with those who keep his covenant and remember to obey his precepts." Your role as a father contributes to a legacy of love that extends to future generations.

Bonding with Your Baby

The chapter we're reading today, "Bonding with Your Baby," is a delightful examination of the extraordinary relationship you'll make with your little one. It's a journey filled with sensitive moments, mutual discovery, and the creation of a friendship that will last a lifetime.

The First Gaze

As a new dad, one of the most profound sensations awaits you in the simple act of staring into your baby's eyes for the first time. It's at these times that you begin to build a connection that goes beyond words. Your infant, in turn, turns to you for comfort and care. This first stare is suggestive of the deep way God looks upon us with love. In Zephaniah 3:17 (NIV), it's said, "The Lord your God is with you, the Mighty Warrior who saves. He will take great delight in you; in his love, he will no longer rebuke you, but will rejoice over you with singing."

Skin-to-Skin Contact

Physical contact plays a critical function in connecting with your kid. The warmth of your embrace, the delicate touch of your hands, and the comfort of your chest create a feeling of security. This closeness is reminiscent of the tender care expressed in Isaiah 40:11 (NIV): "He tends his flock like a shepherd: He gathers the lambs in his arms and carries them close to his heart; he gently leads those that have young." In a similar way, your closeness reassures your baby and fosters a sense of trust.

The Power of Presence

Being present is a fantastic way to connect with your kid. Spend meaningful time together, whether it's during feedings, diaper changes, or just snuggling on the sofa. Ecclesiastes 3:1 (NIV) reminds us of the value of time: "There is a time for everything, and a season for every activity under the heavens." Each minute you spend with your kid is an investment in the relationship you're developing, generating a reservoir of shared memories.

Reading Together

The sound of your voice is a source of comfort for your infant. Reading to your tiny one, even if they're too young to grasp the words, builds a rhythm and familiarity. Consider the words of Proverbs 22:6 (NIV): "Start children off on the way they should go, and even when they are old, they will not turn from it." Reading Scripture or simple tales establishes the groundwork for a love of learning and deepens the link between you and your infant.

Shared Laughter and Joy

Laughter is a global language, and your kid will react to the excitement in your voice and actions. Proverbs 17:22 (NIV) brilliantly encapsulates the effect of joy: "A cheerful heart is good medicine, but a crushed spirit dries up the bones." Your laughing becomes a source of comfort and enjoyment for your infant, providing a pleasant environment that improves your relationship.

Music and Lullabies

Music has a unique way of calming both the psyche and the restless infant. Singing lullabies or playing calm music gives a pleasant background to your baby's environment. Zephaniah 3:17 (NIV) reflects the notion of God singing over us: "He will rejoice over you with singing." In the same manner, your singing produces a melody of love that resonates with your infant, bringing a feeling of security and serenity.

Understanding Cues and Needs

Bonding includes attuning yourself to your baby's indications and demands. As you learn to understand their screams, identify their hunger or sleep signs, you develop your relationship. In the Gospel of Matthew 7:11 (NIV), Jesus illustrates the attentive nature of God: "If you, then, though you are evil, know how to give good gifts to your children, how much more will your Father in heaven give good gifts to those who ask him!" Just as God understands our needs, your attentiveness communicates love and care to your baby.

Navigating Challenges Together

Bonding isn't simply about the pleasant times but also about handling problems together. Colossians 3:13 (NIV) encourages a spirit of forgiveness and patience: "Bear with each other and forgive one another if any of you has a grievance against someone. Forgive as the Lord forgave you." During sleepless nights or fussy moments, your patience and understanding become a testament to the enduring nature of your love.

Building Trust

Trust is the basis of a solid connection. Your regular attention and attentiveness establish a feeling of trust in your infant. Psalm 28:7 (NIV) elegantly depicts the security found in trust: "The Lord is my strength and my shield; my heart trusts in him, and he helps me. My heart leaps for joy, and with my song I praise him." Similarly, your infant finds strength and pleasure in the confidence they put in you as their caretaker.

Creating Rituals and Traditions

Establishing routines and customs offers a feeling of regularity and stability for your infant. Whether it's a nighttime routine, a cherished song, or a morning ritual, these behaviours become anchors in their everyday existence. Proverbs 4:23 (NIV) advises the care of the heart: "Above all else, guard your heart, for everything you do flows from it." Your deliberate rituals become a means of protecting and nurturing the emotional well-being of your kid.

Praying for Your Baby

As a parent, one of the most meaningful ways to connect with your infant is via prayer. Lift up your kid in prayer, requesting God's direction, protection, and blessings. Philippians 4:6-7 (NIV) reassures us about the peace that comes through prayer: "Do not be anxious about anything, but in every situation, by prayer and petition, with thanksgiving, present your requests to God. And the peace of God, which transcends all understanding, will guard your hearts and your minds in Christ Jesus." Your prayers become a source of comfort and grace for both you and your baby.

Reflecting Unconditional Love

Above all, the relationship you have with your infant is a manifestation of unconditional love. 1 Corinthians 16:14 (NIV) advocates love as the guiding principle: "Do everything in love." Your love, expressed through your actions, words, and presence, becomes a strong force influencing your baby's feeling of security and belonging.

===

Emotions of Fatherhood

===

Welcome to the magnificent roller coaster of emotions that is parenting! In this chapter, "Emotions of Fatherhood," we're going to discuss the depth and range of sensations you'll encounter on this journey. From the exciting highs to the hard lows, each feeling is a brushstroke on the canvas of your parenting experience.

- **Joy Beyond Measure:**

One of the first and most intense sensations you'll experience as a new parent is pure, unadulterated joy. The pure thrill of holding your infant, hearing their first scream, and feeling their little fingers wrap around yours is unsurpassed. It's a thrill that parallels the joy expressed in Psalm 127:3 (NIV): "Children are a heritage from the Lord, offspring a reward from him." Your kid is a great gift, and the pleasure they offer is a tribute to the beauty of life.

- **Overwhelming obligation:**

With pleasure comes a profound feeling of obligation. The thought that you are now tasked with the well-being of another human being may be both awe-inspiring and, at times, overwhelming. In Luke 12:48 (NIV), Jesus talks on responsibility: "From everyone who has been given much, much will be demanded; and from the one who has been entrusted with much, much more will be asked." Embracing your job as a parent entails handling the hurdles with a feeling of duty and purpose.

- **Worry and Anxiety:**

It's normal to experience a tinge of worry and anxiety in the middle of this new duty. Will you be a good enough father? Can you supply everything that your kid needs? These worries parallel the emotions described in Philippians 4:6-7 (NIV): "Do not be worried about anything, but in every situation, by prayer and supplication, with thanksgiving, submit your requests to God. And the peace of God, which surpasses all understanding, will protect your hearts and your thoughts in Christ Jesus." Trust in the divine direction as you negotiate the uncertainties of parenting.

- **Unconditional Love:**

The love you feel for your kid is a force unlike any other. It's a love that transcends shortcomings and defies comprehension. 1 Corinthians 13:7 (NIV) nicely expresses the essence of love: "It always protects, always trusts, always hopes, always perseveres." Your love becomes a tower of strength, offering a secure refuge for your kid to develop and prosper.

- **Frustration and Patience:**

Fatherhood comes with its share of problems, and frustration may raise its head. Whether it's dealing with restless nights or interpreting a wailing infant, patience becomes your ally. James 1:19-20 (NIV) implores us to be slow to anger: "My dear brothers and sisters, take note of this: Everyone should be quick to listen, slow to speak and slow to become angry because human anger does not produce the righteousness that God desires." In times of anger, turn to patience and understanding, seeking the direction that leads to righteous answers.

- **Pride in Milestones:**

As your kid reaches developmental milestones, from the first steps to the first words, you'll feel a tremendous sense of pride. Proverbs 23:24 (NIV) expresses the delight of a parent: "The father of a righteous child has great joy; a man who fathers a wise son rejoices in him." Celebrate these milestones as they indicate the development and thriving of the wonderful life you are raising.

- **Sacrificial Love:**

Sacrifice becomes a common concept throughout parenthood. Just as Jesus gave for us, you too will find yourself making sacrifices for the well-being of your kid. Ephesians 5:25 (NIV) talks of sacrificial love: "Husbands, love your wives, just as Christ loved the church and gave himself up for her." Your sacrificial love forms the story of your child's existence and provides a foundation of stability.

- **Guilt and Forgiveness:**

There may be occasions when guilt sneaks in, whether it's missing a milestone or feeling like you should have done better. In these circumstances, recall the forgiveness stressed in Colossians 3:13 (NIV): "Bear with one other and forgive one another if any of you has a grievance against someone. Forgive like the Lord forgave you." Learn from errors, forgive yourself, and push on with a heart devoted to improvement.

- **Amazement and Wonder**:

As you watch your kid discover the world with new eyes, you'll feel a sense of amazement and wonder. This is analogous to the awe stated in Psalm 8:3-4 (NIV): "When I consider your heavens, the work of your fingers, the moon and the stars, which you have set in place, what is mankind that you are mindful of them, human beings that you care for them?" Embrace the surprise of each moment, seeing the divine beauty in the modest actions of discovery.

- **Loneliness and Connection:**

Fatherhood, at times, may seem isolated, particularly in the early years when sleepless nights and unfamiliar habits become the norm. Ecclesiastes 4:9-10 (NIV) extols the benefits of companionship: "Two are better than one, because they have a good return for their labor: If either of them falls down, one can help the other up." Seek connection with other dads, share your stories, and find consolation in the community that knows the unique path you're on.

- **Thankfulness for the Gift of Fatherhood:**

In the middle of all the emotions, express thankfulness for the great gift of fatherhood. Psalm 118:24 (NIV) emphasises an attitude of gratitude: "This is the day the Lord has made; let us rejoice and be glad in it." Each day as a parent is a gift, a chance to accept the variety of emotions and to be present in the extraordinary adventure of leading a new life.

- **Hope for the Future:**

Finally, hang onto hope for the future. Jeremiah 29:11 (NIV) communicates God's plans for us: "For I know the plans I have for you, declares the Lord, plans to prosper you and not to harm you, plans to give you hope and a future." Your journey as a parent is part of a broader design, and your emotions, both highs and lows, add to the rich fabric of this shared trip.

Supporting Your Partner

Let's discuss the essential role you play in being there for your significant other as you both traverse the road of motherhood together. Your support is like a sturdy pillar, offering stability and comfort amid the pleasures and tribulations that come with raising a kid.

- **Recognizing Her Journey:**

The first step in helping your spouse is recognising and respecting the particular journey she is on. Just as God identifies and understands our distinct journeys, as described in Psalm 139:1-3 (NIV): "You have searched me, Lord, and you know me. You know when I sit and when I stand; you detect my thoughts from afar. You distinguish my going out and my laying down; you are acquainted with all my ways." Take the time to be sensitive to your partner's emotions, wants, and experiences.

- **Active Listening:**

One of the most effective methods to give help is via active listening. Proverbs 18:13 (NIV) highlights the necessity of hearing before responding: "To answer before listening—

that is folly and shame." Allow your spouse to share her ideas, worries, and pleasures without interruption. Your careful listening offers a place for open conversation and emotional connection.

- **Empathy and Compassion:**

As your spouse navigates the physical and emotional changes that occur with pregnancy and parenthood, address each circumstance with empathy and compassion. Colossians 3:12 (NIV) invites us to adopt empathy: "Therefore, as God's chosen people, holy and dearly loved, clothe yourselves with compassion, kindness, humility, gentleness, and patience." Your empathetic attitude produces a supportive atmosphere that enhances your partnership.

- **Encouragement and Affirmation:**

Offer words of encouragement and affirmation to elevate your companion. Proverbs 16:24 (NIV) clearly depicts the power of nice words: "Gracious words are a honeycomb, sweet to the soul and healing to the bones." Your good remarks become a source of comfort and strength, forming a foundation of mutual support.

- **Sharing duties:**

Support also means actively sharing duties. Galatians 6:2 (NIV) alludes to the principle of sharing responsibilities: "Carry each other's burdens, and in this way, you will fulfill the law of Christ." Whether it's domestic tasks, infant care, or emotional support, working together enhances your connection and ensures that neither of you feels overwhelmed.

- **Educating Yourself:**

Take the effort to educate yourself about pregnancy, delivery, and parenthood. Proverbs 19:2 (NIV) supports getting knowledge: "Desire without knowledge is not good— how much more will hasty feet miss the way!" Your eagerness to learn displays your dedication to becoming an active and knowledgeable participant.

- **Predicting requirements:**

Be proactive in predicting your partner's requirements. Just as God understands and provides for our needs, 1 Peter 4:10 (NIV) urges us to utilise our talents to serve others: "Each of you should use whatever gift you have received to serve others, as faithful stewards of God's grace in its various forms." Your thoughtful gestures and deeds of service display your love and dedication.

- **Patience in Times of Change:**

Recognize that pregnancy and the early stages of parenthood bring about major changes. Ecclesiastes 3:1 (NIV) comments on the seasons of life: "There is a time for everything, and a season for every activity under the heavens." Exercise patience and adaptation as you both handle the developing dynamics of your relationship and family.

- **Being a Pillar of Strength:**

Your position as a supportive spouse entails being a pillar of strength. Psalm 18:2 (NIV) identifies God as our rock and fortress: "The Lord is my rock, my fortress and my deliverer; my God is my rock, in whom I take refuge, my shield and the horn of my salvation, my stronghold." Similarly, your consistent support provides a source of stability for your relationship during times of uncertainty.

- **Caring for Her Well-being:**

Prioritize your partner's physical and emotional well-being. 1 Corinthians 6:19-20 (NIV) stresses care for our bodies: "Do you not know that your bodies are temples of the Holy Spirit, who is in you, whom you have received from God? You are not your own; you were purchased at a price. Therefore, worship God with your body." Your concern for her well-being recognises the holiness of the life you are fostering together.

- **Establishing Emotional closeness:**

Foster emotional closeness by establishing a safe environment for vulnerability. Proverbs 20:5 (NIV) alludes to the depth of the human heart: "The purposes of a person's heart are deep waters, but one who has insight draws them out." Encourage open conversation, reveal your sentiments, and develop a link that extends beyond the surface.

- **Celebrating successes:**

Celebrate the successes, no matter how minor. Philippians 2:3-4 (NIV) emphasises humility and appreciation of others: "Do nothing out of selfish ambition or pretentious conceit. Rather, in humility value others above yourselves, not looking to your own interests but each of you to the interests of the others." Your shared achievements, whether in parenting or personal accomplishments, increase the feeling of collaboration.

- **Respecting Her Choices:**

Respect your partner's choices and decisions. 1 Peter 3:7 (NIV) encourages mutual respect in marriage: "Husbands, in the same way, be considerate as you live with your wives, and treat them with respect as the weaker partner and as heirs with you of the gracious gift of life so that nothing will hinder your prayers." Mutual respect is the cornerstone of a good and helpful relationship.

Encouraging Self-Care:

Encourage and encourage your spouse in taking time for self-care. Mark 6:31 (NIV) illustrates the significance of rest: "Then, because so many people were coming and going that they did not even have a chance to eat, he said to them, 'Come with me by yourselves to a quiet place and get some rest.'" Recognize the necessity of rest and rejuvenation in maintaining a healthy balance.

- **Getting Help jointly:**

In hard circumstances, be open to getting help jointly. Ecclesiastes 4:9 (NIV) underlines the strength gained in companionship: "Two are better than one, because they have a good return for their labor." Whether via therapy, support groups, or seeking advice from experienced parents, addressing issues together enhances your connection.

- **Expressing thanks:**

Express thanks for your partner's contribution in this shared adventure. 1 Thessalonians 5:18 (NIV) emphasises an attitude of thanksgiving: "Give thanks in all circumstances; for this is God's will for you in Christ Jesus." Your expressions of thanks establish a healthy and grateful climate in your partnership.

- **Embracing Flexibility:**

Flexibility is crucial in negotiating the unexpected nature of parenting. James 1:19 (NIV) emphasises flexibility in listening: "My dear brothers and sisters, take note of this: Everyone should be quick to listen, slow to speak and slow to become angry." Flexibility in your approach provides for adaptation in the face of changing situations.

- **Renewing Intimacy:**

Amidst the pressures of children, prioritize the renewal of intimacy in your partnership. Song of Solomon 4:7 (NIV) praises the beauty of love: "You are altogether beautiful, my darling; there is no flaw in you." Nurture the romantic and personal sides of your relationship, building a stronger connection.

Establishing Routines

As a new parent, you'll quickly learn that routines not only offer order to your days but also create a feeling of security and predictability for both you and your young one.

Understanding the Power of Routines

Think of routines as the compass that governs your day. They're not just about structure; they're about generating a rhythm that offers a feeling of normality to your house. Ecclesiastes 3:1 (NIV) refers to the seasons of life: "There is a time for everything, and a season for every activity under the heavens." Establishing routines helps you manage the varied activities of family life with a feeling of purpose and order.

Setting the Tone for the Day

Morning habits, in particular, may establish a favourable tone for the remainder of the day. Proverbs 27:1 (NIV) advises planning: "Do not boast about tomorrow, for you do not know what a day may bring." While we can't forecast every detail, having a daily routine gives a firm start, decreasing stress and letting you approach the day with purpose.

Creating Consistency for Your Baby

Babies thrive on predictability, and routines give the constancy they need for optimal growth. In Lamentations 3:22-23 (NIV), we find assurance in God's faithfulness: "Because of the Lord's great love we are not consumed, for his compassions never fail. They are new every morning; great is your faithfulness." Your consistency in routines becomes a reflection of the stable love and care your child can depend on.

Establishing Sleep Routines

One of the most critical components of early parenting is establishing sleep habits. Proverbs 3:24 (NIV) recognises the tranquilly found in rest: "When you lie down, you will not be afraid; when you lie down, your sleep will be sweet." Consistent bedtime rituals provide a quiet atmosphere, communicating to your infant that it's time to rest, promoting a feeling of security and restful slumber.

Mealtime Routines and Family Bonding

Mealtime rituals give a fantastic chance for family bonding. In Psalm 34:8 (NIV), we're reminded of the goodness found in coming together: "Taste and see that the Lord is good; blessed is the one who takes refuge in him." Whether it's sharing a meal, expressing gratitude, or enjoying simple conversations, mealtime routines become a sacred space for connection.

Balancing Structure and Flexibility

While routines create structure, it's necessary to balance them with flexibility. James 4:13-15 (NIV) advises humility in planning: "Now listen, you who say, 'Today or tomorrow we will go to this or that city, spend a year there, carry on business and make money.' Why, you do not even know what will happen tomorrow." Being adaptable allows you to embrace the spontaneity of family life while maintaining a foundational routine.

Playtime Routines and Learning

Incorporating playtime patterns is vital for your child's growth. Proverbs 22:6 (NIV) emphasizes the importance of guiding your child: "Start children off on the way they should go, and even when they are old, they will not turn from it." Engaging in consistent playtime routines not only fosters a love for learning but also creates joyful memories for both you and your child.

Incorporating Self-Care Routines

As a new parent, it's tempting to concentrate completely on the routines for your kid. However, don't forget to add self-care practises for yourself and your relationship. Matthew 11:28 (NIV) talks to finding rest in God: "Come to me, all you who are weary and burdened, and I will give you rest." Taking time for self-care helps to your general well-being, enabling you to be completely present for your family.

Navigating Transitions with Ease

Life is riddled with transformations, and routines give a feeling of security amid these changes. Ecclesiastes 3:4 (NIV) acknowledges the ebb and flow of life: "A time to weep and a time to laugh, a time to mourn and a time to dance." During times of change, keeping fundamental routines brings comfort and familiarity, helping your family handle changes with ease.

Teaching Time Management and Responsibility

Routines can act as excellent instruments for teaching time management and responsibility to your kid. Ephesians 5:15-16 (NIV) encourages wise use of time: "Be very careful, then, how you live—not as unwise but as wise, making the most of every opportunity, because the days are evil." Through consistent routines, your child learns to manage their time effectively and develop a sense of responsibility.

Utilizing Naptime Routines

Naptimes are special moments for both your kid and for you. In Mark 6:31 (NIV), Jesus recognizes the importance of rest: "Then, because so many people were coming and going that they did not even have a chance to eat, he said to them, 'Come with me by yourselves to a quiet place and get some rest.'" Naptime routines create a peaceful environment, allowing you to recharge and attend to other tasks.

Building Rituals for Connection

Establishing routines isn't only about efficiency; it's about developing rituals for connection. 1 Thessalonians 5:11 (NIV) emphasises mutual encouragement: "Therefore encourage one another and build each other up, just as in fact you are doing." Whether it's a bedtime tale, a morning stroll, or a weekend tradition, these routines create times of shared delight and connection.

Promoting Independence via Routines

Routines also play a significant part in encouraging independence for your youngster. Galatians 6:4 (NIV) speaks to personal responsibility: "Each one should test their own actions. Then they can take pride in themselves alone, without comparing themselves to someone else." Through routines, your child learns to take ownership of tasks, fostering a sense of accomplishment and independence.

Consistent Discipline within Routines

Discipline is a vital element of parenting, and routines give a foundation for regular discipline. Proverbs 13:24 (NIV) talks to the need of discipline: "Whoever spares the rod hates their children, but the one who loves their children is careful to discipline them." Discipline within routines helps your kid learn limits and expectations, providing a feeling of stability.

Adapting Routines as Your Child Grows

As your kid develops, be prepared to adjust your routines. Ecclesiastes 3:1 (NIV) reminds us of the seasons of life: "There is a time for everything, and a season for every activity under the heavens." Just as the seasons vary, so do the needs and preferences of your kid. Being flexible in altering routines helps them stay relevant and helpful.

Teaching the Value of Order

Routines automatically teach the importance of order and structure. 1 Corinthians 14:40 (NIV) supports orderliness: "But everything should be done in a fitting and orderly way." Through routines, your kid learns the necessity of organization and the comfort that comes from a structured environment.

Fostering a Sense of Security

Above all, routines give a strong feeling of stability for your youngster. Psalm 121:7-8 (NIV) speaks to the Lord as our protector: "The Lord will keep you from all harm— he will watch over your life; the Lord will watch over your coming and going both now and forevermore." Similarly, your consistent routines become a source of security and assurance for your child, creating a stable foundation for their growth.

Chapter 2: Navigating Challenges

Every parent confronts problems, large and little, but it's how you overcome them that forms your journey and builds the relationship with your kid. So, strap up, dad—you've got this.

Expect the Unexpected

First and foremost, be ready for the unexpected. Just as Ecclesiastes 9:11 (NIV) says, "the race is not to the swift or the battle to the strong, nor does food come to the wise or wealth to the brilliant or favor to the learned; but time and chance happen to them all." Life is full of surprises, and parenting is no different. Whether it's a sudden diaper explosion or a restless night, facing the unexpected with resilience can serve you well.

Embracing the Learning Curve

Becoming a parent is like beginning a new job—you're sure to endure a learning curve. Proverbs 18:15 (NIV) advocates an attitude of constant learning: "The heart of the discerning acquires knowledge, for the ears of the wise seek it out." Every problem is a chance to learn, adapt, and develop. Take it one step at a time, and don't be too harsh on yourself while you negotiate this new territory.

Coping with Sleep Deprivation

Ah, sleep deprivation—a rite of passage for every new parent. Psalm 127:2 (NIV) recognises the struggle: "In vain you rise early and stay up late, toiling for food to eat— for he grants sleep to those he loves." While it may feel like you'll never get a full night's sleep again, realise that this period is short. Lean on your support system, take naps when you can, and believe that sleep will return.

Seeking Support from Others

Speaking about assistance, don't hesitate to depend on people. Ecclesiastes 4:9-10 (NIV) emphasizes the strength found in companionship: "Two are better than one, because they have a good return for their labor: If either of them falls down, one can help the other up." Whether it's your partner, friends, or family, a supportive network can make the challenges of fatherhood feel more manageable.

Finding Patience in the Midst of Crying

Babies cry—it's their method of communicating. Finding patience in the middle of those wails might be tricky, but it's vital. James 5:7 (NIV) encourages patience: "Be patient, then, brothers and sisters, until the Lord's coming. See how the farmer waits for the land to yield its valuable crop, patiently waiting for the autumn and spring rains." Just like a farmer waits for the harvest, your patience during crying spells will yield moments of peace.

Balancing Work and Family

Navigating the delicate balance between work and family life is a difficulty many parents encounter. Colossians 3:23 (NIV) relates to the devotion we should bring to our job: "Whatever you do, work at it with all your heart, as working for the Lord, not for human masters." While work is vital, achieving that balance is key. Prioritize quality time with your family, and remember that the moments you share are valuable.

Maintaining Your Relationship

The nature of your relationship with your spouse may vary with the advent of a kid. Ephesians 4:2-3 (NIV) highlights qualities that can strengthen relationships: "Be completely humble and gentle; be patient, bearing with one another in love. Make every effort to keep the unity of the Spirit through the bond of peace." Navigating this shift requires open communication, understanding, and a joint effort to maintain the bond that brought you together in the first place.

Cultivating Resilience

Resilience is a crucial attribute in parenthood. Proverbs 24:16 (NIV) acknowledges that the righteous may fall, but they rise again: "for though the righteous fall seven times, they rise again, but the wicked stumble when calamity strikes." Embrace challenges as opportunities for growth, and let resilience be your guide as you face the inevitable ups and downs of parenting.

Learning to Let Go

As a parent, you'll rapidly recognise the significance of flexibility and learning to let go of control. Proverbs 19:21 (NIV) refers to the sovereignty of God's intentions: "Many are the plans in a person's heart, but it is the Lord's purpose that prevails." Sometimes, things won't go according to plan, and that's good. Adapting to the unexpected and letting go of strict expectations will make the trip smoother.

Dealing with Parenting Differences

It's normal for you and your spouse to have different parenting techniques. Ecclesiastes 4:12 (NIV) illustrates the strength of unity: "Though one may be overpowered, two can defend themselves. A cord of three strands is not quickly broken." Work together, establish common ground, and respect the variety of your ideas. Your kid benefits from the balance established by both parents.

Managing Financial Pressures

The financial duties of motherhood may be frightening. Philippians 4:19 (NIV) gives reassurance: "And my God will meet all your needs according to the riches of his glory in Christ Jesus." While it's vital to plan and budget, believe that, with effort and faith, you can handle the financial difficulties that come with having a kid.

Facing Health Challenges

Sometimes, health issues may develop, either for your kid or yourself. Isaiah 41:10 (NIV) is a source of comfort in such times: "So do not fear, for I am with you; do not be dismayed, for I am your God. I will strengthen you and help you; I will uphold you with my righteous right hand." Seek support from healthcare professionals, stay resilient, and remember that you're not alone in facing health challenges.

Dealing with Sibling Rivalry

As your family expands, so may sibling rivalry. Proverbs 17:17 (NIV) supports love in tough situations: "A friend loves at all times, and a brother is born for a time of adversity." Help your children create strong relationships by promoting love and understanding among siblings. Teach dispute resolution and demonstrate the patience and kindness you hope to see in them.

Cultivating a Healthy Self-Care Routine

In the middle of parenting issues, don't forget to care for yourself. 1 Corinthians 6:19-20 (NIV) reminds us of the importance of self-care: "Do you not know that your bodies are temples of the Holy Spirit, who is in you, whom you have received from God? You are not your own; you were bought at a price. Therefore, honor God with your bodies." Prioritize your physical and mental well-being, knowing that a well-rested and rejuvenated parent is better equipped to face challenges.

Embracing the Imperfect Moments

Perfection is an unattainable aim in motherhood. 2 Corinthians 12:9 (NIV) speaks to God's grace in our weakness: "But he said to me, 'My grace is sufficient for you, for my power is made perfect in weakness.' Therefore, I will boast all the more gladly about my weaknesses, so that Christ's power may rest on me." Embrace the imperfect moments, knowing that they are opportunities for growth and connection with your child.

Teaching Problem-Solving Skills

Challenges are fantastic chances to teach your youngster problem-solving abilities. James 1:5 (NIV) recommends seeking knowledge: "If any of you lacks wisdom, you should ask God, who gives generously to all without finding fault, and it will be given to you." Involve your kid in finding answers to daily issues, strengthening their independence and problem-solving ability.

Building a Support Network

Building a solid support network is vital in handling problems. Proverbs 11:14 (NIV) stresses the knowledge found in a plurality of counselors: "For lack of guidance a nation falls, but victory is won through many advisers." Seek assistance from experienced parents, friends, and relatives. Their thoughts and shared experiences might give helpful perspectives as you approach issues together.

Teaching Resilience to Your Child

Just as you create resilience within yourself, conveying this attribute to your kid is vital. Romans 5:3-4 (NIV) speaks to the growth that comes through perseverance: "Not only so, but we also glory in our sufferings, because we know that suffering produces perseverance; perseverance, character;

and character, hope." Teach your child that challenges are stepping stones to growth and resilience.

Fostering a Positive Mindset

Maintain an optimistic outlook in the face of adversities. Philippians 4:8 (NIV) provides guidance on our thought patterns: "Finally, brothers and sisters, whatever is true, whatever is noble, whatever is right, whatever is pure, whatever is lovely, whatever is admirable—if anything is excellent or praiseworthy—think about such things." Cultivating a positive outlook contributes to your resilience and the atmosphere in your home.

Modeling Emotional Expression

It's crucial to model appropriate emotional expression for your kid. Ecclesiastes 3:4 (NIV) recognises the varied emotions we experience: "a time to weep and a time to laugh, a time to mourn and a time to dance." Allow your kid to understand that it's good to exhibit a variety of emotions, and teach them appropriate strategies to navigate and deal with hard feelings.

Reaching Out for Professional Help

In certain circumstances, issues may need expert help. Proverbs 15:22 (NIV) underscores the benefit of obtaining advice: "Plans fail for lack of counsel, but with many advisers, they succeed." Whether it's parenting courses, counseling, or therapy, reaching out for professional assistance is a proactive and prudent move in conquering obstacles.

Learning from Mistakes

It's natural to make errors along the road. Proverbs 24:16 (NIV) acknowledges that the righteous may fall, but they rise again: "for though the righteous fall seven times, they rise again, but the wicked stumble when calamity strikes." Learn from your mistakes, grow through them, and let them become stepping stones to becoming a wiser and more compassionate father.

Maintaining a Sense of Humor

Lastly, don't forget to preserve a sense of humor. Proverbs 17:22 (NIV) acknowledges the therapeutic influence of laughter: "A cheerful heart is good medicine, but a crushed spirit dries up the bones." Laughter may be a strong cure to the trials of parenthood. Find delight in the simple moments, and allow humor be a companion on your parenthood journey.

"Navigating Challenges" is a vital aspect of the fabric of parenthood. Every struggle is a chance for development, resilience, and greater relationships with your kid. Remember, you're not alone on this road, and with each struggle comes the chance for a better and more rewarding bond with your little one. Embrace the trials, learn from them, and allow them develop you into the amazing parent you are supposed to be.

Sleepless Nights

Ah, restless nights — the rite of passage for any new parent. Welcome to the midnight realm of parenting, when the moon becomes your buddy and your baby's screams choreograph the music of your evenings. As you begin on this path, it's crucial to accept the problems of insomnia with kindness, understanding, and a dash of humor.

The Symphony of Cries

Picture this: it's 2 a.m., and you find yourself in a dimly lighted room, swaying gently with your darling infant in your arms. The lullabies play quietly in the background while your baby's screams fill the air. In such times, it's easy to feel a mix of tiredness and perplexity. Ecclesiastes 3:1 (NIV) whispers to your exhausted heart: "There is a time for everything, and a season for every activity under the heavens." These restless nights are merely a season, a fleeting moment in the magnificent tapestry of parenthood.

Navigating the New Normal

Sleepless nights become your new normal, and handling them needs a recalibration of expectations. Proverbs 3:24 (NIV) brings solace: "When you lie down, you will not be afraid; when you lie down, your sleep will be sweet." lovely sleep may seem like a faraway dream today, but believe that this transition is short. Your infant is learning to navigate the world, and your reassuring presence in the tiny hours is their assurance.

Finding Rhythms in the Darkness

Amidst the restless haze, locate patterns that provide solace. Just like Psalm 42:8 (NIV) alludes about the Lord's song being with us throughout the night, establish your own calming rhythms. Whether it's a gentle swing, a lullaby, or a muttered prayer, these rituals become anchors in the darkness, establishing a feeling of comfort for both you and your tiny one.

The Unseen Bond in the Night

In the silence of the night, as the world sleeps, a special kinship emerges. 1 Corinthians 13:7 (NIV) brilliantly describes the core of this connection: "It always protects, always trusts, always hopes, always perseveres." In the silence of the night, your presence becomes a shield, and your persistence in soothing your infant establishes a foundation of trust and hope.

The Power of Shared Responsibilities

Navigating restless nights is a shared duty. Galatians 6:2 (NIV) advocates sharing one another's responsibilities: "Carry each other's burdens, and in this way, you will fulfill the law of Christ." Whether you take turns with your spouse or seek help from family, the shared weight becomes lighter. A unified front in facing the issues of insomnia improves your connection as parents.

Resilience in the Midnight Hour

Resilience becomes your buddy at the midnight hour. Romans 5:3-4 (NIV) speaks to the character forged through perseverance: "Not only so, but we also glory in our sufferings because we know that suffering produces perseverance; perseverance, character; and character, hope." Embrace the challenges of sleepless nights as opportunities for personal and familial growth.

Navigating the Fog of Exhaustion

Exhaustion becomes a common friend during restless nights. Matthew 11:28 (NIV) provides a calming invitation: "Come to me, all you who are weary and burdened, and I will give you rest." While a full night's sleep may be hard, find times to rest and recharge throughout the day. Seeking help from loved ones assists you to traverse the veil of weariness with more ease.

Embracing the Stillness for Reflection

Amidst the night's calm, discover moments for meditation. Psalm 4:4 (NIV) advises us to "Tremble and do not sin; when you are on your beds, search your hearts and be silent." Use the peaceful hours for self-reflection, thankfulness, and appreciating the particular privileges that come with the trials of motherhood.

Cultivating a Grateful Heart

In the middle of restless nights, nurture a thankful heart. 1 Thessalonians 5:18 (NIV) fosters an attitude of thanksgiving: "Give thanks in all circumstances; for this is God's will for you in Christ Jesus." Find thankfulness in the simple moments - the warmth of your infant in your arms, the softness of their breath, and the honour of being their parent.

Embracing the Beauty of the Night

While the night may feel unending, there's a distinct beauty in its quietude. Song of Solomon 2:8 (NIV) portrays the voice of the beloved as "leaping over the mountains, bounding over the hills." In the silence of the night, appreciate the beauty of the link you have with your infant. These moments, albeit tough, are infused with an incredible pleasure.

Remaining Present in the Darkness

It's natural to pine for the early light during restless nights, yet there's beauty in staying present in the darkness. Psalm 139:11-12 (NIV) acknowledges God's omnipresence: "If I say, 'Surely the darkness will hide me and the light become night around me,' even the darkness will not be dark to you; the night will shine like the day, for darkness is as light to you." In your presence, even the darkest hours can shine with love and tenderness.

Seeking Wisdom in the Night Watches

The night watches become a time for seeking knowledge. Proverbs 4:7 (NIV) urges us: "The beginning of wisdom is this: Get wisdom. Though it cost all you have, get understanding." In the quietude of the night, seek wisdom in parenting literature, shared experiences, and the intuition that increases with each reassuring hug.

Honoring Your Role as a Protector

As you traverse restless nights, remember your job as a guardian. Psalm 17:8 (NIV) nicely depicts this sentiment: "Keep me as the apple of your eye; hide me in the shadow of your wings." In the silence of the night, you are the shelter, the defender, and the reassuring presence that your infant seeks consolation in.

The Beauty of Early Morning Moments

As darkness transforms to day, savour the beauty of early morning hours. Psalm 30:5 (NIV) tells us that "weeping may stay for the night, but rejoicing comes in the morning." With the first light, there's a feeling of achievement, a new day packed with options, and the promise of rest on the horizon.

Creating a Sleep-Friendly Environment

In your trek through restless nights, build a sleep-friendly atmosphere. Proverbs 3:24 (NIV) supports tranquil rest: "When you lie down, you will not be afraid; when you lie down, your sleep will be sweet." Dim the lights, maintain a suitable temperature, and set relaxing bedtime practises to ease your infant into the quiet night.

Being Kind to Yourself

Amidst the hardships, be gentle to yourself. Ephesians 4:32 (NIV) speaks to kindness: "Be kind and compassionate to one another, forgiving each other, just as in Christ God forgave you." Parenting is a process filled with learning, and there's grace in realising that perfection is not the objective. Be compassionate to yourself as you negotiate the twists and turns of restless nights.

Creating a Support System

Building a support system is vital during restless nights. Ecclesiastes 4:12 (NIV) shows the strength found in unity: "Though one may be overpowered, two can defend themselves. A cord of three strands is not quickly broken." Seek support from your spouse, family, and friends. Knowing you're not alone makes the road more tolerable.

Remembering that It's Just a Season

Above all, remember that restless nights are merely a season. Ecclesiastes 3:1 (NIV) brilliantly illustrates the spirit of seasons: "There is a time for everything, and a season for every activity under the heavens." This tough period will change, and as you weather the night together, a fresh morning awaits.

Balancing Work and Family

The delicate dance of managing work and family—the persistent difficulty for many men. Welcome to the ever-evolving balance of obligations, where your position as a provider crosses with your path as a parent. As you walk into this complicated balancing act, realise that you're not alone, and there's wisdom to be found in both experience and timeless texts.

Understanding the Tension

The strain between job and family is as ancient as time. Ecclesiastes 3:1 (NIV) brilliantly illustrates the ebb and flow of life: "There is a time for everything, and a season for every activity under the heavens." Recognize that your life encompasses several seasons, each needing its share of attention. Balancing work and family is about navigating these seasons with insight and judgement.

Prioritizing What Matters Most

In the middle of deadlines and diaper changes, it's vital to prioritize what matters most. Matthew 6:33 (NIV) gives a timeless guideline: "But seek first his kingdom and his righteousness, and all these things will be given to you as well." Prioritize your connection with God, your family, and your work—in that order. When your priorities are aligned, the balancing act becomes a more conscious and purpose-driven exercise.

Creating Boundaries

Boundaries are your hidden weapon in the realm of juggling work and family. Proverbs 4:23 (NIV) implores us to watch our hearts: "Above all else, guard your heart, for everything you do flows from it." Establishing clear boundaries between work and family time ensures that each element of your life gets the attention it needs. When you're at work, be totally present; when you're with your family, let work take a back seat.

Embracing Quality Over Quantity

In the pursuit for balance, adopt the credo of quality above quantity. Psalm 90:12 (NIV) challenges us to "Teach us to number our days, that we may gain a heart of wisdom." Be purposeful with your time. It's not about the shear quantity of time you spend but the quality of the experiences you make. Make the most of the time you have with your family, relishing each valuable connection.

Being Present in the Moment

Being present in the moment is a gift you offer to both your job and your family. Colossians 3:23 (NIV) stresses giving your best: "Whatever you do, work at it with all your heart, as working for the Lord, not for human masters." Whether you're tackling a job assignment or playing with your kid, bring your entire heart to the moment. The advantages of true presence are incalculable.

Fostering Open Communication

Communication is the cornerstone in managing work and family. Proverbs 15:22 (NIV) extols the significance of asking advice: "Plans fail for lack of counsel, but with many advisers, they succeed." Talk frankly with your spouse about your professional responsibilities, expectations, and family aspirations. A common knowledge guarantees that you're on the same page and can negotiate the delicate balance together.

Setting Realistic Expectations

Setting reasonable expectations is crucial to preventing burnout. Proverbs 16:9 (NIV) tells us that "In their hearts, humans plan their course, but the Lord establishes their steps." While it's wise to plan, allow space for divine direction. Be realistic about what you can do both at work and at home. A deliberate approach provides for a more sustainable and enjoyable journey.

Creating Rituals of Connection

Rituals of connection anchor your family in the middle of a hectic world. Ecclesiastes 4:12 (NIV) underscores the strength found in unity: "Though one may be overpowered, two can defend themselves. A cord of three strands is not quickly broken." Whether it's a weekly family dinner, a bedtime routine with your child, or a regular date night with your partner, these rituals create a sense of connection that transcends the demands of daily life.

Incorporating Flexibility

Flexibility is your ally in the balancing act. James 4:13-15 (NIV) promotes humility in planning: "Now listen, you who say, 'Today or tomorrow we will go to this or that city, spend a year there, carry on business and make money.' Why, you do not even know what will happen tomorrow." Be open to the twists and turns life may offer. A flexible attitude helps you to adjust to unanticipated events without losing your balance.

Embracing the Concept of Seasons

Understanding the notion of seasons is a game-changer. Ecclesiastes 3:1 (NIV) tells us: "There is a time for everything, and a season for every activity under the heavens." There will be seasons of severe job demands and seasons when family takes first. Recognize the ebb and flow, and change your priorities appropriately. Embracing the cycle of seasons offers a feeling of balance to your life.

Balancing Self-Care

In the search of balance, don't forget about self-care. 1 Corinthians 6:19-20 (NIV) highlights the sanctity of our bodies: "Do you not know that your bodies are temples of the Holy Spirit, who is in you, whom you have received from God? You are not your own; you were bought at a price. Therefore, honor God with your bodies." Taking care of your physical and mental well-being is not selfish; it's a responsibility that allows you to show up fully for both your work and your family.

Seeking Wisdom from Others

Seeking counsel from others is a sign of strength, not weakness. Proverbs 13:10 (NIV) alludes to the benefit of asking guidance: "Where there is strife, there is pride, but wisdom is found in those who take advice." Connect with experienced dads, mentors, or coworkers who have successfully traversed the landscape of work and family. Their thoughts may give useful perspectives and direction.

Embracing the Power of No

Learning to say no is a vital skill in the balancing act. Proverbs 16:9 (NIV) tells us that "In their hearts, humans plan their course, but the Lord establishes their steps." While it's easy to take on every opportunity that comes your way, assess what corresponds with your objectives and beliefs. Saying no when required ensures that your obligations stay in alignment with your larger aims.

Building a Support System

Building a support system is equivalent to having a safety net. Ecclesiastes 4:9-10 (NIV) highlights the power gained in companionship: "Two are better than one, because they have a good return for their labor: If either of them falls down, one can help the other up." Surround yourself with helpful coworkers, friends, and family. Knowing you have a network to draw on makes the balancing task more doable.

Understanding the Impact of Presence

Your presence carries enormous significance in both your job and your family. Ephesians 5:15-16 (NIV) instructs us to

"Be very careful, then, how you live—not as unwise but as wise, making the most of every opportunity." Your presence at work helps to your professional advancement, while your presence at home moulds the relationships with your family. Be diligent about making the most of every opportunity.

Modeling a Healthy Work Ethic

Modeling a strong work ethic is a crucial lesson for your children. Colossians 3:23-24 (NIV) stresses the significance of working with excellence: "Whatever you do, work at it with all your heart, as working for the Lord, not for human masters, because you know that you will receive an inheritance from the Lord as a reward. It is the Lord Christ you are serving." Your dedication to greatness creates a legacy for the generations to come.

Acknowledging and Learning from Mistakes

Mistakes are unavoidable in the search of equilibrium. Proverbs 24:16 (NIV) admits that "though the righteous fall seven times, they rise again, but the wicked stumble when calamity strikes." Learn from your failures, change your approach, and let them be stepping stones toward a more harmonious and rewarding balance between work and family.

Cultivating Gratitude for the Journey

Cultivating appreciation for the trip turns the balancing act into a wonderful experience. 1 Thessalonians 5:18 (NIV) urges us to "Give thanks in all circumstances; for this is God's will for you in Christ Jesus." Express thankfulness for the chances your career gives, for the times with your family, and for the development that comes with the delicate dance of balancing both.

Leaving Room for Joy in Each Role

In the balancing act, allow space for delight in each role you perform. Psalm 16:11 (NIV) speaks to the fullness of joy found in God's presence: "You make known to me the path of life; you will fill me with joy in your presence, with eternal pleasures at your right hand." Whether at work or at home, infuse joy into your tasks, knowing that each role contributes to the richness of your life.

Embracing the Journey, Not Just the Destination

Lastly, enjoy the journey, not just the goal. Proverbs 19:21 (NIV) refers to the sovereignty of God's plans: "Many are the plans in a person's heart, but it is the Lord's purpose that prevails." While you may have goals for both your profession and your family, be open to the twists and turns that God's purpose reveals. The trip itself contains great lessons and moments of grace.

The skill of managing work and family is a subtle ballet, a symphony of duties that, when performed with knowledge and elegance, produces a peaceful existence. As you begin on this path, remember that it's not about reaching a perfect balance at every time but about navigating the many seasons with purpose and love. Your devotion to both your career and your family is a tribute to the depth of your life. May your path be blessed with moments of pleasure, satisfaction, and the insight to handle the delicate dance of work and family with grace.

===

Dealing with Uncertainty

===

The unexplored seas of doubt — a common companion in the adventure of parenting. As you walk into this job, realise that coping with uncertainty is part and parcel of the experience. It's like beginning on a road trip without a map, navigating the twists and turns with both dread and exhilaration. Let's uncover the art of confronting the unknown with confidence, faith, and a heart ready for whatever is ahead.

The Nature of Uncertainty

Uncertainty, my friend, is stitched into the fabric of existence. Proverbs 16:9 (NIV) presents a clear picture: "In their hearts, humans plan their course, but the Lord establishes their steps." As a new parent, you may have goals and ambitions, but the road ahead frequently develops in unexpected ways. Embracing uncertainty is not a sign of weakness; rather, it's an awareness that life's path is a vast tapestry of surprises.

The Adventure of Parenthood

Welcome to the magnificent adventure of parenting, where uncertainty takes center stage. James 4:14 (NIV) reflects on the fleeting nature of life: "Why, you do not even know what will happen tomorrow. What is your life? You are a mist that appears for a little while and then vanishes." Parenthood is a journey filled with unpredictability, a beautiful dance between planning and surrendering to the unknown.

Embracing a Spirit of Flexibility

In the face of uncertainty, create an attitude of adaptability. Proverbs 19:21 (NIV) shows the sovereignty of God's plans: "Many are the plans in a person's heart, but it is the Lord's purpose that prevails." While you may have goals for parenting, be open to the divine diversions and surprises that come your way. Flexibility permits you to manage unpredictability with grace and resilience.

Trusting the Divine Navigator

In the sea of uncertainty, trust the Divine Navigator. Proverbs 3:5-6 (NIV) gives timeless guidance: "Trust in the Lord with all your heart and lean not on your own understanding; in all your ways submit to him, and he will make your paths straight." Trust that even amid uncertainty, there's a supernatural hand orchestrating the trip. Lean into that faith, knowing that every twist and turn has a reason.

Navigating the Unknown with Wisdom

While uncertainty abounds, navigate the unknown with knowledge. Proverbs 2:6 (NIV) alludes to the source of genuine wisdom: "For the Lord gives wisdom; from his mouth come knowledge and understanding." Seek wisdom in your parenting journey — from experienced parents, from reliable resources, and from your own thoughts. Wisdom is a guiding light in the face of ambiguity.

Finding Comfort in God's Presence

In times of uncertainty, take comfort in God's presence. Joshua 1:9 (NIV) assures: "Have I not commanded you? Be strong and courageous. Do not be afraid; do not be discouraged, for the Lord your God will be with you wherever you go." God's presence is a stable anchor amid the turbulent seas of uncertainty. Take consolation in the knowing that you're not alone on this road.

Embracing the Process of Growth

Uncertainty is not simply a difficulty; it's a chance for progress. Romans 5:3-4 (NIV) beautifully captures this truth: "Not only so, but we also glory in our sufferings, because we know that suffering produces perseverance; perseverance, character; and character, hope." As you navigate the uncertainties of fatherhood, recognize that each challenge is a stepping stone to personal and familial growth.

Learning to Let Go

Dealing with uncertainty frequently entails mastering the skill of letting go. Matthew 6:34 (NIV) gives a significant perspective: "Therefore do not worry about tomorrow, for tomorrow will worry about itself. Each day has enough trouble of its own." Release the grasp on excessive concern about the future. Focus on the now, relishing the time with your kid, and trust that tomorrow will unfold as it should.

Embracing a Positive Mindset

Maintain an optimistic outlook in the face of uncertainty. Philippians 4:8 (NIV) provides a guide for our thoughts: "Finally, brothers and sisters, whatever is true, whatever is noble, whatever is right, whatever is pure, whatever is lovely, whatever is admirable—if anything is excellent or praiseworthy—think about such things." Cultivate a positive outlook, finding joy in the small moments and opportunities for growth in the challenges.

Modeling Resilience for Your Child

As you encounter uncertainty, demonstrate resilience for your youngster. James 1:12 (NIV) speaks to the blessing of perseverance: "Blessed is the one who perseveres under trial because, having stood the test, that person will receive the crown of life that the Lord has promised to those who love him." Your resilience becomes a powerful example, showing your child how to navigate life's uncertainties with strength and grace.

Creating a Support System

Building a support system is a lifeline in uncertain times. Ecclesiastes 4:9-10 (NIV) extols the strength found in companionship: "Two are better than one, because they have a good return for their labor: If either of them falls down, one can help the other up." Surround yourself with supportive friends, relatives, and fellow parents. Share your doubts and seek direction, understanding that a shared weight is lighter.

Embracing the Beauty of Unplanned Moments

Within the domain of uncertainty lies the beauty of unanticipated moments. Psalm 139:16 (NIV) acknowledges the intricacy of God's design: "Your eyes saw my unformed body; all the days ordained for me were written in your book before one of them came to be." Embrace the joy that comes with the unexpected – the spontaneous laughter, the unplanned adventures, and the surprises that make fatherhood a rich tapestry.

Acknowledging Your Limitations

It's fair to admit your limits in the midst of uncertainty. 2 Corinthians 12:9-10 (NIV) speaks to God's grace in our weaknesses: "But he said to me, 'My grace is sufficient for you, for my power is made perfect in weakness.' Therefore, I will boast all the more gladly about my weaknesses, so that Christ's power may rest on me." Surrender your limitations to God's grace, allowing His strength to shine through your vulnerabilities.

Teaching Adaptability to Your Child

As you negotiate uncertainty, offer the crucial skill of flexibility to your kid. Proverbs 19:20 (NIV) encourages us to listen to advice and accept discipline: "Listen to advice and accept discipline, and at the end you will be counted among the wise." Teach your child the importance of adapting to changing circumstances, learning from experiences, and approaching uncertainties with a teachable spirit.

Cultivating a Heart of Gratitude

Cultivate a heart of thankfulness despite uncertainty. 1 Thessalonians 5:16-18 (NIV) encourages a spirit of thanksgiving: "Rejoice always, pray continually, give thanks in all circumstances; for this is God's will for you in Christ Jesus." In moments of uncertainty, express gratitude for the blessings that surround you – the love of your family, the beauty of life, and the opportunities for growth.

Turning Uncertainty into an Opportunity for Trust

Uncertainty gives a unique chance to develop your confidence in God. Proverbs 3:5-6 (NIV) beautifully guides us: "Trust in the Lord with all your heart and lean not on your own understanding; in all your ways submit to him, and he will make your paths straight." Let uncertainty be a catalyst for surrender, trusting that God's plan is more intricate and purposeful than we can fathom.

Drawing Strength from Prayer

In uncertain times, gain strength from the power of prayer. Philippians 4:6-7 (NIV) assures us: "Do not be anxious about anything, but in every situation, by prayer and petition, with thanksgiving, present your requests to God. And the peace of God, which transcends all understanding, will guard your hearts and your minds in Christ Jesus." Prayer becomes a sanctuary of peace in the midst of uncertainty.

Celebrating the Gift of Today

Amidst the uncertainty of tomorrow, cherish the gift of today. Psalm 118:24 (NIV) tells us to celebrate in the present: "This is the day the Lord has made; let us rejoice and be glad in it." Cherish the moments with your kid, appreciating the beauty of today. In doing so, you fill each day with thankfulness and excitement, regardless of what tomorrow may contain.

Patience in Parenthood

Let's unravel the art of patience in motherhood, a path packed with situations that will test, refine, and eventually deepen the reservoirs of your patience.

- **The Gentle Art of Waiting:**

Patience in motherhood is the delicate skill of waiting. Ecclesiastes 7:8 (NIV) rightly notes, "The end of a matter is better than its beginning, and patience is better than pride." In the early days and nights of parenthood, you'll confront problems that may seem overwhelming. Remember, the path of motherhood unfolds gradually, and the beauty of it resides in the process. Have patience as you observe the development, the first smiles, and the milestones that characterise your child's journey.

- **Nurturing Seeds of Understanding:**

Patience fosters seeds of enlightenment. James 1:19 (NIV) offers timeless advice: "My dear brothers and sisters, take note of this: Everyone should be quick to listen, slow to speak and slow to become angry." In the whirlwind of parenthood, take a moment to truly listen – to your partner, to your child's cues, and to the wisdom of experience.

Patience permits you to comprehend the needs of your family and react with love and empathy.

- **Facing the Unexpected with Calmness:**

Parenthood is packed with unexpected twists and turns. Proverbs 14:29 (NIV) emphasises a calm spirit: "Whoever is patient has great understanding, but one who is quick-tempered displays folly." When confronted with unforeseen obstacles – whether it a diaper explosion, a late-night feeding, or a toddler's tantrum – address them with composure. Your calm manner provides a soothing salve in the face of the uncertain.

- **Guiding with a Gentle Hand:**

Patience is the kind hand that leads. Ephesians 4:2 (NIV) speaks to the core of patience: "Be completely humble and gentle; be patient, bearing with one another in love." As a parent, your instruction develops the character of your kid. Whether you're teaching a new skill, navigating conflicts, or instilling values, do so with a gentle hand and a patient heart. The seeds you plant today will blossom in the years to come.

- **Creating a Sanctuary of Calm**:

In the middle of the commotion that might accompany motherhood, establish a refuge of peace with patience. Philippians 4:6-7 (NIV) reminds us of the peace that comes with prayer: "Do not be anxious about anything, but in every situation, by prayer and petition, with thanksgiving, present your requests to God. And the peace of God, which transcends all understanding, will guard your hearts and your minds in Christ Jesus." Patience in prayer becomes a source of tranquility amidst the whirlwind of parenting.

- **Responding to Milestones with Joy:**

Parenthood is characterised by innumerable milestones — the first steps, the first words, and all the minor wins that unfurl. Galatians 6:9 (NIV) urges us to persevere: "Let us not become weary in doing good, for at the proper time we will reap a harvest if we do not give up." Celebrate these milestones with pleasure and patience, knowing that each step, no matter how little, is a testimonial to your child's progress.

- **Navigating Sleepless Nights with Grace:**

Ah, the notorious restless nights - a characteristic of early fatherhood. 1 Thessalonians 5:14 (NIV) speaks to supporting one another: "And we urge you, brothers and sisters, warn those who are idle and disruptive, encourage the disheartened, help the weak, be patient with everyone." In the haze of sleep deprivation, be patient with your partner, with yourself, and with your little one. These evenings are simply a season, and with patience, you'll traverse them with grace.

- **Building Trust Through Consistency:**

Consistency is the cornerstone of creating trust with your kid. Proverbs 22:6 (NIV) gives timeless wisdom: "Start children off on the way they should go, and even when they are old, they will not turn from it." By being consistently patient in your replies, you create a foundation of trust. Your kid learns that you are a stable presence, always there with love, understanding, and patience.

- **Weathering the Storms Together:**

Parenting, just like life, has its storms. Matthew 8:26 (NIV) highlights the power of faith amidst storms: "He replied, 'You of little faith, why are you so afraid?' Then he got up and rebuked the winds and the waves, and it was completely calm." Be the calm in the storm for your family. With patience, you can weather hardships together, emerging stronger and more unified.

- **Learning from the Journey:**

Patience allows you to be a continual student on this road of motherhood. Proverbs 19:20 (NIV) urges us to seek advise: "Listen to advice and accept discipline, and at the end, you will be counted among the wise." Seek assistance from experienced parents, learn from your child's signs, and embrace the lessons that patience teaches you along the road. Each moment, whether easy or tough, is a chance for development.

- **Modeling Emotional Regulation:**

Your child looks to you as a model for emotional control. James 1:19-20 (NIV) stresses self-control: "My dear brothers and sisters, take note of this: Everyone should be quick to listen, slow to speak and slow to become angry, because human anger does not produce the righteousness that God desires." Model the art of patience in controlling emotions, teaching your kid the vital ability of self-control.

- **Encouraging Independence with Patience:**

As your kid develops, promote independence with patience. Galatians 5:22-23 (NIV) defines the fruit of the Spirit: "But the fruit of the Spirit is love, joy, peace, forbearance, kindness, goodness, faithfulness, gentleness, and self-control." Patience, or patience, is a fundamental ingredient in establishing independence. Allow your kid to explore, make mistakes, and learn, guiding them with tolerance and love.

- **Instilling a Love for Learning:**

Patience and a desire for learning go hand in hand. Proverbs 2:2-5 (NIV) speaks to the pursuit of knowledge: "turning your ear to wisdom and applying your heart to understanding—indeed, if you call out for insight and cry aloud for understanding, and if you look for it as for silver and search for it as for hidden treasure, then you will understand the fear of the Lord and find the knowledge of

God." Instill in your youngster the delight of discovery, cultivating a patient curiosity that lasts a lifetime.

- **Creating a Culture of Encouragement:**

Patience develops a culture of encouragement among your family. 1 Thessalonians 5:11 (NIV) supports building each other up: "Therefore encourage one another and build each other up, just as in fact you are doing." When obstacles occur, be patient with your child's attempts, expressing words of encouragement. Your encouragement becomes a source of strength, creating a powerful character in your little one.

- **Balancing Boundaries with Compassion:**

Establishing limitations is crucial in parenting, and patience helps you balance them with compassion. Colossians 3:12 (NIV) refers to the relevance of compassion: "Therefore, as God's chosen people, holy and dearly loved, clothe yourselves with compassion, kindness, humility, gentleness, and patience." Set hard boundaries with compassion, expressing them gently to your youngster. In doing so, you transmit key lessons while retaining a connection founded on understanding.

- **Enjoying the Present Moment:**

Amidst the hustle of parenthood, enjoy the present moment with patience. Ecclesiastes 3:1 (NIV) wonderfully expresses the essence of time: "There is a time for everything, and a season for every activity under the heavens." Whether it's a tranquil time with your youngster, a boisterous laughter, or a shared narrative before sleep, be entirely present. Patience helps you to enjoy the beauty of each vanishing moment.

- **Fostering Resilience Through Challenges:**

Challenges are inescapable in parenting, and patience becomes a catalyst for growing resilience. Romans 12:12 (NIV) emphasises perseverance: "Be joyful in hope, patient in affliction, faithful in prayer." When presented with adversities, handle them with patience, establishing in your youngster the tenacity to endure and the confidence that they can overcome hurdles with grace.

- **Recognizing the Unique Journey of Each Child:**

Patience pushes you to recognise the unique journey of each youngster. Psalm 139:13-14 (NIV) acknowledges the complexity of God's creation: "For you formed my inmost being; you knit me together in my mother's womb. I applaud you because I am fearfully and wonderfully formed; your works are marvellous, I know that full well." Each kid is fearfully and wonderfully designed, with a particular path to unfurl. Patience enables you to recognise and nurture the distinctiveness of each small one.

- **Cultivating a Legacy of Love:**

In the fabric of parenthood, patience builds a legacy of love. 1 Corinthians 13:4-7 (NIV) clearly depicts the essence of love: "Love is patient, love is kind. It does not envy, it does not brag, it is not boastful. It does not disrespect others, it is not self-seeking, it is not quickly angry, it maintains no record of wrongs. Love does not pleasure in wickedness but rejoices with the truth. It always defends, always trusts, always hopes, always perseveres." Patience is an expression of love — a love that protects, trusts, hopes, and perseveres through the seasons of motherhood.

- **Resting in the Assurance of God's Timing:**

Above all, rest in the confidence of God's timetable. Ecclesiastes 3:11 (NIV) effectively articulates this truth: "He has created everything lovely in its time. He has also implanted eternity in the human heart; but no one can grasp what God has done from beginning to end." Your path as a dad unfolds in God's perfect time. Trust that each moment, with its struggles and delights, is a part of a broader plan that unfolds wonderfully.

Coping with Stress

Welcome to a subject that's as ubiquitous as it is challenging: dealing with stress. As a new or soon-to-be parent, you're embarking into a job that's both extremely gratifying and, at times, rather demanding. Stress is like an undesirable acquaintance that might turn up unannounced. But worry not, because in the middle of the turmoil, there's a route to serenity. Let's go into the art of managing with stress in this changing season of life.

- **The Nature of Stress:**

Stress is the heavy load we all wear, full with the anxieties, expectations, and uncertainties of life. It's a regular guest in the domain of new motherhood. Philippians 4:6-7 (NIV) presents a timeless perspective: "Do not be worried about anything, but in every circumstance, by prayer and supplication, with thanksgiving, submit your requests to God. And the peace of God, which surpasses all understanding, will protect your hearts and your thoughts in Christ Jesus." Recognize that it's good to be anxious, but also realise that you don't have to carry the weight alone.

- **Piloting the Storms:**

Parenthood frequently seems like piloting a ship during storms, with waves of responsibility slamming from every direction. Matthew 8:23-27 (NIV) gives a striking image of managing storms: "Then he got into the boat and his followers followed him. Suddenly a fierce storm sprang up on the lake such that the waves rushed over the boat. But Jesus was asleep. The disciples ran and awakened him, begging, 'Lord, rescue us! We're going to drown!' He said, 'You of little faith, why are you so afraid?' Then he stood up and rebuked the winds and the seas, and everything was absolutely peaceful." In the storms of stress, turn to your anchor, whether it's prayer, a supportive spouse, or close friends.

- **Understanding Stress Triggers:**

Identifying stress triggers is like locating the roots of a plant. Proverbs 12:25 (NIV) recognises the weight of anxiety: "Anxiety weighs down the heart, but a kind word cheers it up." Take a time to concentrate on what exactly creates stress for you. Is it lack of sleep, financial problems, or the expectation to be a great parent? Understanding these triggers helps you to handle them more effectively.

- **Embracing Self-Care:**

Self-care is not a luxury; it's a need, particularly amid the frenzy of new parenthood. 1 Corinthians 6:19-20 (NIV) gives insight on the significance of caring for oneself: "Do you not know that your bodies are temples of the Holy Spirit, who is in you, whom you have received from God? You are not your own; you were purchased at a price.

Therefore worship God with your body." Prioritize your physical and emotional well-being. Whether it's a peaceful time with a book, a stroll in nature, or a good night's sleep — embrace self-care as a method to rejuvenate.

- **Building a Support System:**

No man is an island, particularly in the arena of parenting. Ecclesiastes 4:9-10 (NIV) talks to the power found in companionship: "Two are better than one, because they have a good return for their labor: If either of them falls down, one can help the other up." Surround yourself with a support system — friends, family, other parents – who understand the experience. Sharing the burden makes the weight of stress more tolerable.

- **Setting Realistic Expectations:**

The expectations we set on ourselves, sometimes greater than the responsibilities we bear. Proverbs 16:9 (NIV) gives a viewpoint on planning: "In their hearts humans plan their course, but the Lord establishes their steps." While preparing for your family's future is vital, remember that flexibility and adaptability are virtues. Set reasonable expectations, knowing that perfection is not the objective, but rather, a path of development and learning.

- **Prioritizing and Organizing:**

In the turmoil of motherhood, prioritize and organize like a seasoned captain charting a course. 1 Corinthians 14:40

- **(NIV) promotes order:**

"But everything should be done in a fitting and orderly way." Establish routines, prioritize things, and split them into manageable stages. This not only assists in controlling stress but also guarantees that your focus is directed toward what genuinely important.

- **Practicing Mindfulness:**

Mindfulness is a strong weapon in the struggle against stress. Philippians 4:8 (NIV) gives a guidance for our thoughts: "Finally, brothers and sisters, whatever is true, whatever is noble, whatever is right, whatever is pure, whatever is lovely, whatever is admirable—if anything is excellent or praiseworthy—think about such things." Train your mind to concentrate on the current moment rather than being overwhelmed by future problems.

- **Finding delight in tiny Moments:**

Amidst the tension, find delight in the tiny moments. Ecclesiastes 3:12-13 (NIV) recognises the basic pleasures of life: "I know that there is nothing better for people than to be happy and to do good while they live. That everyone of them may eat and drink, and find contentment in all their toil—this is the gift of God." Whether it's a baby's grin, a shared joke, or a quiet moment of introspection, cherish these tiny delights as gifts in the midst of life's responsibilities.

- **Balancing Work and Family:**

Balancing work and family is a tightrope walk that many men endure. Colossians 3:23-24 (NIV) talks to the value of labour: "Whatever you do, work at it with all your heart, as working for the Lord, not for human masters, because you know that you will receive an inheritance from the Lord as a reward. It is the Lord Christ you are serving." While aiming for greatness in your profession, also ensure that you carve out devoted, quality time for your family.

- **Learning to Say No:**

The power of saying no is frequently underestimated. Proverbs 16:7 (NIV) talks about pleasing the Lord: "When the Lord takes pleasure in anyone's way, he causes their enemies to make peace with them." Learn to say no to responsibilities that strain you too thin. Prioritize your well-being and the well-being of your family above the urge to satisfy everyone.

- **Seeking Professional assistance:**

In the process of managing with stress, seeking professional assistance is a show of strength, not weakness. Proverbs 11:14 (NIV) relates to the wisdom found in seeking counsel: "For lack of guidance a nation falls, but victory is won through many advisers." Whether it's a counselor, therapist, or a support group, obtaining professional assistance may give essential insights and ways to handle stress successfully.

- **Prayer as a Source of Strength:**

In situations of stress, turn to prayer as a source of strength. Philippians 4:13 (NIV) reinforces this truth: "I can do all this through him who gives me strength." Pour out your heart in prayer, seeking wisdom, serenity, and strength from the One who knows the depths of your troubles. In the quiet times of prayer, you may encounter a calm that beyond comprehension.

- **Focusing on What You Can Control:**

Life is packed with circumstances beyond our control. James 4:13-15 (NIV) presents a viewpoint on planning: "Now listen, you who say, 'Today or tomorrow we will move to this or that city, spend a year there, carry on business and earn money.' Why, you do not even know what will happen tomorrow. What is your life? You are a cloud that emerges for a brief time and then fades." Focus on what you can control — your actions, responses, and the choices you make in the now.

- **Accepting Imperfection:**

Accepting imperfection is a liberating step in dealing with stress. Matthew 5:48 (NIV) reminds us of our human limitations: "Be perfect, therefore, as your heavenly Father is perfect." Embrace the truth that you are human, and imperfection is part of the human experience. Release the weight of perfection and give yourself the grace to grow and learn from the problems you meet.

- **Building Resilience Through Challenges:**

Challenges are not hurdles but chances for progress. Romans 5:3-4 (NIV) brilliantly encapsulates this truth: "Not only so, but we also glory in our sufferings, because we know that suffering produces perseverance; perseverance, character; and character, hope." Embrace adversity as a route to resilience. Each difficulty you endure has the ability to develop you into a better, more resilient parent.

- **Celebrating accomplishments, Big and little:**

Amidst the tension, take time to appreciate accomplishments, big and little. Psalm 118:24 (NIV) tells us to celebrate in the present: "This is the day the Lord has made; let us rejoice and be glad in it." Whether it's effectively calming a fussy infant, accomplishing a hard assignment, or just making it through a chaotic day, recognise these wins as milestones on your path.

- **Connecting with Your spouse:**

In the dance of motherhood, your spouse is your most vital dancing partner. Ecclesiastes 4:12 (NIV) alludes to the strength of partnership: "Though one may be overcome, two may protect themselves. A string of three strands is not rapidly broken." Share your worries, encourage each other, and draw on the strength of your relationship. Together, you can weather the storms and relish the pleasures.

- **Reflecting on thankfulness:**

In the midst of stress, ponder on thankfulness. 1 Thessalonians 5:18 (NIV) emphasises an attitude of thanksgiving: "Give thanks in all circumstances; for this is God's will for you in Christ Jesus." Even at hard circumstances, discover things of your life to be thankful for - the love of your family, the support of friends, and the opportunity for development. Gratitude becomes a beacon of light in the darkest of circumstances.

- **Embracing the pleasure of parenthood:**

Amidst the hustle and bustle, never lose sight of the pleasure that parenthood gives. Psalm 127:3 (NIV) wonderfully defines children as a legacy and a reward: "Children are a heritage from the Lord, offspring a reward from him." hug the delight in your child's laughing, the warmth of their hug, and the priceless moments that make the struggles worthwhile.

Chapter 3: Building Strong Connections

Today, let's go into a subject that is as crucial as the oxygen we breathe — developing strong relationships with your young one. As you hold that beautiful bundle in your arms, you're going into a position that's not only about giving but also about building ties that endure a lifetime. So, let's examine the skill of developing solid connections, a foundation that will mould the wonderful tapestry of your relationship with your kid.

- **The Power of Presence:**

In the hustle and bustle of life, the simple act of being present says volumes. Ecclesiastes 3:1 (NIV) brilliantly illustrates the essence of time: "There is a time for everything, and a season for every activity under the heavens." Embrace the seasons of your child's life with your full attention. Whether it's participating in play, sharing a meal, or just being there in quiet times, your presence creates the framework for a deep bond.

- **Quality Over number:**

It's not about the number of time you spend with your kid but the quality of those times. Psalm 90:12 (NIV) gives a helpful perspective on time: "Teach us to number our days, that we may gain a heart of wisdom." Treasure each moment, relishing the depth of connection that comes from being totally present. A brief, concentrated conversation may frequently make a more lasting impact than hours of unfocused presence.

- **Listening with Intent:**

The art of connection starts with listening. James 1:19 (NIV) gives timeless advice: "My dear brothers and sisters, take note of this: Everyone should be quick to listen, slow to speak and slow to become angry." Listen to your kid with focus, not only to their words but to the feelings and needs underneath the surface. The simple act of being heard builds a feeling of trust and understanding.

- **Shared Moments of delight:**

Find delight in the shared moments — laughing, play, and the simple joys of life. Proverbs 17:22 (NIV) shows the significance of joy: "A cheerful heart is good medicine, but a crushed spirit dries up the bones." Create a reservoir of shared delight with your kid, whether it's via amusing pranks, shared travels, or experiencing the world together. These moments form the building blocks of a deep bond.

- **Building Trust Through Consistency:**

Consistency is the cornerstone of trust. Proverbs 3:3-4 (NIV) talks to the significance of trust: "Let love and fidelity never leave you; wrap them around your neck, record them on the tablet of your heart. Then you will acquire favor and a good reputation in the eyes of God and man." Be constant in your reactions, in your presence, and in the love you offer. Trust is developed via the dependability of your conduct.

- **Cultivating a Safe area:**

Your connection with your kid is a sanctuary, a safe area where they may express themselves without fear of judgment. Proverbs 14:26 (NIV) talks to the shelter found in a strong connection: "Whoever fears the Lord has a secure fortress, and for their children, it will be a refuge." Cultivate an atmosphere where your kid feels secure to discuss their ideas, aspirations, and anxieties. In doing so, you develop a bond that withstands the tests of time.

- **The Language of Love**:

Love is a language that transcends words. 1 Corinthians 16:14 (NIV) underlines the power of love: "Do everything in love." Express your affection for your kid not just via words but through your deeds. Whether it's a reassuring embrace, a shared smile, or a helpful hand, let your love be a physical force that reinforces the links between you.

- **Understanding Their Unique Language:**

Just as you communicate love, comprehend the unique language of your kid. Proverbs 22:6 (NIV) promotes understanding their individuality: "Start children off on the way they should go, and even when they are old, they will not turn from it." Pay attention to their signals, their hobbies, and the intricacies of their personality. Each kid is unique, and knowing their language builds a relationship that connects with their heart.

- **Affirmation and Encouragement:**

Affirmation and encouragement are strong instruments in establishing confidence and connection. 1 Thessalonians 5:11 (NIV) talks about building each other up: "Therefore encourage one another and build each other up, just as in fact, you are doing." Celebrate your child's successes, no matter how minor. Your words of encouragement become a source of strength and a monument to your steadfast support.

- **Celebrating Their Individuality:**

Each kid is fearfully and wonderfully formed. Psalm 139:13-14 (NIV) acknowledges the complexity of God's creation: "For you formed my inmost being; you knit me together in my mother's womb. I applaud you because I am fearfully and wonderfully formed; your works are marvellous, I know that full well." Celebrate the individuality of your kid — their abilities, idiosyncrasies, and the wonderful tapestry that makes them who they are. By appreciating their uniqueness, you deepen the relationship that transcends time.

- **Creating Rituals and Traditions:**

Rituals and traditions create a feeling of continuity and warmth into your connection. Ecclesiastes 3:1 (NIV) recognises the seasons of life: "There is a time for everything, and a season for every activity under the heavens." Whether it's a bedtime tale, a weekly game night, or a unique handshake, these rituals build shared experiences that bond you and your kid together.

- **Teaching Through Shared Values:**

As a parent, you are not simply a provider but a guide. Deuteronomy 6:6-7 (NIV) alludes to the function of teaching: "These commands that I tell you today are to be on your hearts. Impress them on your children. Talk about them when you sit at home and when you go down the road, when you lay down and when you get up." Share your ideals, your principles, and the lessons you've learnt. Through these shared beliefs, you teach not only information but a feeling of identity and belonging.

- **Patience as a Virtue:**

In the ebb and flow of parenting, patience becomes a virtue that sustains your bond. Colossians 3:12 (NIV) alludes to the necessity of patience: "Therefore, as God's chosen people, holy and dearly loved, clothe yourselves with compassion, kindness, humility, gentleness, and patience." Be patient with your child's development, their obstacles, and the process of creating a solid bond. Patience promotes resilience and strengthens the roots of your connection.

- **Embracing teaching Moments:**

Life is a series of teaching moments. Proverbs 1:8-9 (NIV) underlines the significance of parental guidance: "Listen, my son, to your father's guidance and do not abandon your mother's teaching. They are a garland to decorate your head and a chain to adorn your neck." Embrace these times as chances to convey knowledge, values, and life lessons. Your instruction becomes a compass that helps your kid navigate the intricacies of the world.

- **Adapting to Their Changing Needs:**

As your kid develops, so do their needs. Ephesians 6:4 (NIV) promotes adaptation in parenting: "Fathers, do not exasperate your children; instead, bring them up in the training and instruction of the Lord." Be alert to their shifting needs — emotionally, socially, and spiritually. Your flexibility generates an atmosphere where people feel understood and supported.

- **Leading by Example:**

Your deeds speak louder than words. 1 Timothy 4:12 (NIV) supports leadership by example: "Don't let anyone look down on you because you are young, but set an example for the believers in speech, in conduct, in love, in faith and in purity." Model the beliefs and habits you intend to establish in your kid. Your example provides a guide for people to follow, establishing the relationship via shared beliefs.

- **Navigating Challenges Together:**

Life is not without its problems, and managing them together deepens the connections of connection. Galatians 6:2 (NIV) talks about carrying each other's responsibilities: "Carry each other's burdens, and in this way, you will fulfill the law of Christ." Be a source of support and consolation in times of struggle. Your desire to tackle obstacles together promotes resilience and enhances your bond.

- **Apologizing and Forgiving:**

In the path of developing relationships, the capacity to apologize and forgive is a healing salve. Colossians 3:13 (NIV) promotes forgiveness: "Bear with one other and forgive one another if any of you has a grievance against someone. Forgive like the Lord forgave you." Acknowledge your faults, apologize when appropriate, and demonstrate the mercy of forgiveness. These behaviours develop a culture of humility and love inside your partnership.

- **Praying for Your kid:**

As a parent, one of the most significant gifts you can offer your kid is your prayers. Philippians 4:6-7 (NIV) relates to the power of prayer: "Do not be worried about anything, but in every circumstance, by prayer and supplication, with thanksgiving, submit your requests to God. And the peace of

God, which surpasses all understanding, will protect your hearts and your thoughts in Christ Jesus." Lift your kid in prayer, requesting direction, protection, and blessings for their path.

- **Embracing Unconditional Love:**

Above all, let your relationship be founded in unconditional love. 1 Corinthians 13:4-7 (NIV) nicely depicts love: "Love is patient, love is kind. It does not envy, it does not brag, it is not boastful. It does not disrespect others, it is not self-seeking, it is not quickly angry, it maintains no record of wrongs. Love does not pleasure in wickedness but rejoices with the truth. It always defends, always trusts, always hopes, always perseveres." Your unconditional love forms a foundation that withstands the challenges of time, hardships, and successes.

Playtime with Your Baby

Welcome to one of the most pleasant chapters of parenting — fun with your kid. As you traverse the early days of motherhood, participating in play with your young one is not just about fun and games; it's a deep method to form ties, promote growth, and create lasting memories. So, let's enter into the realm of playfulness, where laughter, learning, and love interweave.

- **The Language of Play:**

Did you know that play is a universal language for babies? It's how kids explore, learn, and communicate. Jesus recognized the purity of a child's heart in Matthew 18:3 (NIV): "Truly I tell you, unless you change and become like little children, you will never enter the kingdom of heaven." In play, your baby invites you into their world, and as you embrace the simplicity of their joy, you're tapping into something beautiful.

- **Infant Play: The Basics:**

In the early months, your baby's world focuses on sensory encounters. Soft rattles, soft music, and high-contrast toys catch their interest. Proverbs 20:12 (NIV) brilliantly speaks to the miracles of perception: "Ears that hear and eyes that see—the Lord has made them both." Create a sensory-rich environment, exploring textures, sounds, and sights with your infant. These basic encounters help to their cognitive growth.

- **Tummy Time Adventures:**

Ah, the adventure of tummy time! It may seem like a tiny achievement, but it's a key component of your baby's growth. Psalm 139:14 (NIV) recognises the complexity of creation: "I praise you because I am fearfully and wonderfully made; your works are wonderful, I know that full well." During belly time, your baby acquires strength, develops motor skills, and learns to investigate their environment. Join them on their trip, giving support and gentle play to make the experience joyful.

- **Peekaboo and Beyond:**

Peekaboo — a classic game that spans generations. Luke 11:9 (NIV) encourages persistence: "So I say to you: Ask and it will be given to you; seek and you will find; knock and the door will be opened to you." Much like the anticipation in peekaboo, your baby begins to understand object permanence – the idea that things exist even when they can't be seen. Extend the delight by playing hide-and-seek with toys, developing a feeling of curiosity and discovery.

- **Interactive Storytime:**

Storytime isn't simply for sleep; it's an engaging component of playtime. Proverbs 22:6 (NIV) alludes to the effect of early experiences: "Start children off on the way they should go, and even when they are old, they will not turn from it." Choose basic board books with brilliant illustrations and engage your infant with energetic narrative. Let children touch and feel the textures of the book, making reading an engaging and pleasant experience.

- **Music and Movement:**

There's something amazing about the mix of music and movement. Ecclesiastes 3:4 (NIV) acknowledges the rhythm of life: "a time to weep and a time to laugh, a time to mourn and a time to dance." Create a playlist of calm melodies, sway to the beat, and watch how your baby reacts to the pleasure of music. This not only boosts their aural awareness but also creates the framework for future dance parties with your young one.

- **Exploring the Great Outdoors:**

Nature is a playground ready to be explored. Genesis 2:15 (NIV) underlines our responsibilities as stewards of God's creation: "The Lord God took the man and put him in the Garden of Eden to work it and take care of it." Take your infant outside for a breath of fresh air. Feel the grass, marvel at the foliage, and let your baby discover the marvels of the world. Nature becomes a canvas for inquiry and discovery.

- **Building Block Adventures:**

As your infant develops, enter the domain of building blocks. 1 Corinthians 3:9 (NIV) likens ourselves to God's building: "For we are co-workers in God's service; you are God's field, God's building." Stack, knock down, and rebuild together. It's not just about the blocks; it's about developing a foundation of creativity, problem-solving, and cooperation. Your infant learns cause and effect, spatial awareness, and the delight of making something with your aid.

- **Water Play Fun:**

Bath time isn't only about getting clean; it's a chance for water play enjoyment. Isaiah 12:3 (NIV) wonderfully compares pleasure to pulling water from wells: "With joy, you will draw water from the wells of salvation." Invest in a few bath toys, generate moderate waves, and watch as your baby splashes, laughs, and finds the love of water. It's a sensory-rich experience that adds a fun aspect to your everyday routine.

- **Puppetry Magic:**

Enter the wonderful realm of puppetry. Ecclesiastes 3:4 (NIV) acknowledges the joy of laughter: "a time to weep and a time to laugh, a time to mourn and a time to dance." Simple sock puppets or plush animal buddies may become active characters in your playing experiences. Your infant not only appreciates the visual stimulation but also learns to comprehend the notion of engagement and narrative.

- **Mirror, Mirror:**

A mirror is like a wonderful gateway for your infant. 1 Corinthians 13:12 (NIV) uses the metaphor of a mirror to describe our understanding: "For now we see only a reflection as in a mirror; then we shall see face to face. Now I know in part; then I shall know fully, even as I am fully known." Set up a baby-safe mirror and let your little one explore their reflection. It's not simply play; it's a fascinating voyage of self-discovery.

- **Gentle Sensory Play:**

Engage in sensory play that stimulates your baby's senses. Colossians 2:6-7 (NIV) encourages growth in faith: "So then, just as you received Christ Jesus as Lord, continue to live your lives in him, rooted and built up in him, strengthened in the faith as you were taught, and overflowing with thankfulness." Create a sensory bin with safe materials like rice, pasta, or fabric. Let your infant explore diverse textures, building a sense of touch and curiosity.

- **The Magic of Puzzles:**

Puzzles may seem like a big-kid pastime, but even the smallest hands may appreciate the enchantment of simple puzzles. Proverbs 2:6 (NIV) recognises the source of wisdom: "For the Lord gives wisdom; from his mouth come knowledge and understanding." Choose puzzles with big, easy-to-grasp pieces. As you lead your infant in putting parts together, you're not simply playing; you're establishing the framework for problem-solving abilities.

- **Dance Party Extravaganza:**

Turn your living room into a dancing floor! Zephaniah 3:17 (NIV) vividly shows God's joy: "The Lord your God is with you, the Mighty Warrior who saves. He will take great delight in you; in his love, he will no longer rebuke you but will rejoice over you with singing." Play music, hug your baby close, and dance together. Your motions become a source of joy, laughter, and a celebration of the simple joys of life.

- **Imaginary Play Adventures:**

As your infant matures into toddlerhood, start on imagined play experiences. Proverbs 23:24 (NIV) praises the pleasure of parenting: "The father of a righteous child has great joy; a man who fathers a wise son rejoices in him." Whether it's pretending to cook in a little kitchen, having a tea party, or embarking on a make-believe trip, join their world with excitement. Your involvement not only drives their creativity but also improves the link between you.

- **Balancing Solo and Joint Play:**

Encourage both solo and collaborative play. Ecclesiastes 4:9-10 (NIV) highlights the strength found in companionship: "Two are better than one, because they have a good return for their labor: If either of them falls down, one can help the other up." While independent play fosters self-sufficiency, joint play creates shared memories and strengthens your connection. Strike a balance between both, acknowledging the benefit each offers to your baby's growth.

- **The Gift of Laughter:**

Laughter is a global language that transcends age. Proverbs 17:22 (NIV) recognises the power of joy: "A cheerful heart is good medicine, but a crushed spirit dries up the bones." Embrace the gift of laughing in your playtime relationships. Whether it's goofy faces, hilarious noises, or tickle battles, your laughing becomes a source of delight that resonates with your kid.

- **Capturing Everyday Moments:**

Remember, playtime isn't only about organised activities; it's about catching ordinary moments. Psalm 118:24 (NIV) invites us to rejoice in the present: "This is the day the Lord has made; let us rejoice and be glad in it." Whether it's a spontaneous game of peekaboo during diaper changes or making funny faces during mealtime, these impromptu interactions become cherished memories woven into the fabric of your relationship.

Creating Family Traditions

Today, let's go on a great trip — the art of building family traditions. As you enter into the role of a father, you have the unique opportunity to create the culture of your family, weaving threads of love, joy, and shared experiences into the fabric of your life. Family traditions are like the glue that ties hearts together, producing a feeling of connection and treasured memories. So, let's explore the beauty of developing traditions that will become the lifeblood of your family.

- **The Significance of Family Traditions:**

Family traditions are the memorable events, the rituals, and the customs that define your family's identity. Proverbs 4:1-4 (NIV) refers to the knowledge handed down through generations: "Listen, my sons, to a father's instruction; pay attention and gain understanding. I give you sound learning, so do not forsake my teaching."

Think of traditions as the glue that ties your family. They create a feeling of continuity, stability, and shared ideals. Whether it's a simple bedtime routine, a holiday custom, or a monthly family activity, these moments form a foundation that your children will take with them throughout their lives.

- **Starting Small:**

Traditions don't need to be complicated; they may start with the simplest of gestures. Genesis 8:22 (NIV) underlines the permanence of seasons: "As long as the earth endures, seedtime and harvest, cold and heat, summer and winter, day and night will never cease."

Consider beginning with a weekly family lunch, maybe a scheduled night when everyone gets together, shares a meal, and reviews their week. It might be a time for laughing, storytelling, and just being present with one another. This little custom may be the cornerstone around which you construct more complicated family rituals.

- **Celebrating Milestones:**

Milestones, both large and little, are chances to make lasting memories. Joshua 4:6-7 (NIV) talks of placing up stones as a memorial: "In the future, when your children ask you, 'What do these stones mean?' tell them that the flow of the Jordan was cut off before the ark of the covenant of the Lord."

When your kid hits a milestone, whether it a birthday, a graduation, or even a personal success, celebrate it as a family. Create traditions around these occasions - maybe a special dinner, a family excursion, or a passionate letter expressing your pride and affection. These ceremonies not only memorialise the event but also underline the value of family support and togetherness.

- **Holiday Traditions:**

Holidays provide a rich field for creating family customs. Deuteronomy 16:14 (NIV) talks about enjoying holidays with your family: "Be joyful at your festival—you, your sons and daughters, your male and female servants, and the Levites, the foreigners, the fatherless and the widows who live in your towns."

Whether it's Christmas, Thanksgiving, Hanukkah, or any other festival, build traditions that connect with the spirit of the occasion. It may be decorating the home together, creating a special dinner, or participating in acts of kindness. These customs generate a feeling of unity and make holidays more memorable.

- **Daily Rituals:**

In the hustle and bustle of everyday life, discover moments for daily routines. Psalm 119:105 (NIV) compares God's word to a candle for our feet: "Your word is a lamp for my feet, a light on my path."

Consider integrating a daily routine, maybe a bedtime tale, a moment of thanks around the dinner table, or a morning prayer. These simple but constant routines establish anchor points in your child's day, creating a feeling of stability and connection.

- **Cultural Traditions:**

If your family has cultural origins, accept and cherish them. Leviticus 19:32 (NIV) relates on respecting the old: "Stand up in the presence of the aged, show respect for the elderly and revere your God. I am the Lord."

Share tales, create traditional dishes, and participate in activities that represent your ethnic history. This not only instills a feeling of pride in your child's individuality but also ties them to a greater cultural tapestry.

- **Outdoor Adventures:**

Nature itself may be a canvas for family rituals. Genesis 1:31 (NIV) recognises the excellence of God's creation: "God saw all that he had made, and it was very good."

Whether it's a monthly trek, an annual camping trip, or a simple Sunday afternoon nature stroll, these outdoor activities become beloved memories. They not only nurture a passion for the outdoors but also give opportunity for bonding and shared experiences.

- **Acts of Kindness:**

Teaching compassion and kindness is a precious gift. Ephesians 4:32 (NIV) emphasises love and forgiveness: "Be kind and compassionate to one another, forgiving each other, just as in Christ God forgave you."

Incorporate acts of compassion into your family rituals. It may be volunteering together, engaging in community service, or initiating random acts of kindness as a family. These rituals build a feeling of empathy and thankfulness in your children, turning them into caring humans.

- **Tech-Free Time:**

In a society overrun by technology, designate tech-free time as a family custom. Ecclesiastes 3:1 (NIV) refers to the seasons of life: "There is a time for everything, and a season for every activity under the heavens."

Whether it's a weekly game night, a device-free supper, or an hour of unplugged family time, these traditions offer room for true interactions. They enable your family to be present with each other without the distractions of electronics.

- **Documenting Memories:**

Capture the spirit of your family's journey by capturing memories. Habakkuk 2:2 (NIV) talks about writing down visions: "Then the Lord replied: 'Write down the revelation and make it plain on tablets so that a herald may run with it.'"

Create traditions around capturing significant experiences — maybe a family diary where everyone participates, an annual picture book, or a specific area for exhibiting artwork and souvenirs. These customs build a visual narrative of your family's story.

- **Inclusive Traditions:**

Ensure that your family customs are inclusive and adaptive. Romans 12:16 (NIV) urges living in harmony: "Live in harmony with one another. Do not be proud, but be willing to associate with people of low position. Do not be conceited."

Consider the unique tastes and interests of each family member. Your traditions should be flexible enough to suit everyone, generating a feeling of inclusion and belonging.

- **Legacy-Building Traditions:**

Think beyond the present — build traditions that add to your family's heritage. Proverbs 13:22 (NIV) talks about leaving an inheritance: "A good person leaves an inheritance for their children's children, but a sinner's wealth is stored up for the righteous."

Whether it's passing along a favourite family recipe, adopting a family motto, or planting a tree together, these traditions give a feeling of continuity. They remind your children that they are part of something larger than themselves.

Communication with Your Partner

Today, let's dig into a critical facet of motherhood — communication with your spouse. As you negotiate the thrilling path of parenthood, keeping open and efficient communication with your significant other becomes a cornerstone for a happy family. It's not only about sharing words; it's about developing a solid foundation of understanding, trust, and cooperation. So, take a seat, and let's study the art of communicating in this great experience called motherhood.

- **The Power of Words:**

Words are powerful. They have the potential to build up or take down. Proverbs 15:1 (NIV) rightly states, "A gentle answer turns away wrath, but a harsh word stirs up anger." As you begin on this parenting path, remember that the way you speak sets the tone for your family. Choose phrases that elevate, encourage, and build a feeling of oneness.

- **Active Listening:**

Communication is a two-way street, and active listening is the key. James 1:19 (NIV) gives helpful advice: "My dear brothers and sisters, take note of this: Everyone should be quick to listen, slow to speak and slow to become angry." When your spouse is expressing their views or worries, give them your entire attention. Listen not only to reply, but to comprehend. This creates an atmosphere where both of you feel heard and respected.

- **Expressing Your Feelings:**

Don't be hesitant to express your emotions honestly. Ephesians 4:15 (NIV) recommends telling the truth in love: "Instead, speaking the truth in love, we will grow to become in every respect the mature body of him who is the head, that is, Christ." Share your joys, worries, and even your uncertainties. Honest and vulnerable conversation increases your connection and enriches your relationship.

- **Choosing the Right Time:**

Timing matters in communication. Proverbs 25:11 (NIV) eloquently shows this: "Like apples of gold in settings of silver is a ruling rightly given." Choose the perfect moment to address critical topics. Avoid difficult chats while emotions are high or when there are distractions. Finding a quiet and comfortable setting ensures that your talks are productive and solutions-oriented.

- **Non-Verbal Communication:**

Communication isn't simply about words; non-verbal signals play a crucial role. 1 Peter 3:3-4 (NIV) highlights the beauty of a gentle spirit: "Your beauty should not come from outward adornment, such as elaborate hairstyles and the wearing of gold jewelry or fine clothes. Rather, it should be that of your inner self, the unfading beauty of a gentle and quiet spirit, which is of great worth in God's sight." Be mindful of your body language and facial expressions – they convey messages that can either enhance or hinder understanding.

- **Resolving Conflicts:**

Conflict is a normal part of every relationship, but it's how you manage it that counts. Matthew 18:15 (NIV) gives a template for conflict resolution: "If your brother or sister sins, go and point out their fault, just between the two of you. If they listen to you, you have won them over." When problems occur, handle them gently and quietly. Focus on finding solutions rather than assigning blame, and remember that you're a team working towards the same objective — a happy and healthy family.

- **Using "I" Statements:**

"I" statements may be a game-changer in communication. Instead of saying, "You always do this," try saying, "I feel this way when this happens." Philippians 2:3 (NIV) encourages humility: "Do nothing out of selfish ambition or vain conceit. Rather, in humility value others above yourselves." This approach fosters understanding and promotes a collaborative mindset, reducing defensiveness and opening the door to constructive dialogue.

- **Appreciation & Encouragement:**

Never underestimate the power of recognition and encouragement. 1 Thessalonians 5:11 (NIV) advises us to encourage one another: "Therefore encourage one another and build each other up, just as in fact, you are doing." Acknowledge your partner's efforts, whether great or little. Expressing thanks fosters a pleasant environment and supports the concept that you're in this together.

- **Shared Responsibilities:**

Communication is crucial when it comes to distributing tasks. Galatians 6:2 (NIV) stresses sharing each other's loads: "Carry each other's burdens, and in this way, you will fulfill the law of Christ." Discuss and arrange how you'll divide parenting tasks, home work, and other obligations. Having a clear understanding eliminates misunderstandings and develops a feeling of collaboration.

- **Setting Goals Together:**

Communication is crucial in defining and accomplishing mutual objectives. Proverbs 16:3 (NIV) promotes committing plans to the Lord: "Commit to the Lord whatever you do, and he will establish your plans." Whether it's financial objectives, parenting tactics, or job ambitions, speak about your vision for the future. When you're on the same page, you can work together towards establishing the life you both want.

- **Quality Time:**

Amidst the rush of motherhood, prioritize quality time together. Song of Solomon 7:11-12 (NIV) speaks of the beauty of love: "Come, my beloved, let us go to the countryside, let us spend the night in the villages. Let us go early to the vineyards to see if the vines have budded, if their blossoms have opened, and if the pomegranates are in bloom—there I will give you my love." Whether it's a date night, a weekend getaway, or even a quiet evening at home, invest in moments that strengthen your connection.

- **Checking In Regularly:**

Life goes swiftly, and things change. Regular check-ins are crucial. Proverbs 27:23 (NIV) talks to understanding the state of your flocks: "Be sure you know the condition of your flocks, give careful attention to your herds." In the context of family life, this involves being alert to each other's needs, worries, and pleasures. Regularly checking in ensures that you're both maturing together in your responsibilities as parents and spouses.

- **Seeking Support Together:**

Don't hesitate to seek help jointly when required. Ecclesiastes 4:12 (NIV) highlights the strength in numbers: "Though one may be overpowered, two can defend themselves. A cord of three strands is not quickly broken." Whether it's seeking advice from trusted friends, joining a parenting class, or seeking the guidance of a counselor, facing challenges together strengthens your bond.

- **Apologizing and Forgiving:**

Every relationship faces bumps along the road, and learning how to apologize and forgive is vital. Colossians 3:13 (NIV) emphasises forgiveness: "Bear with each other and forgive one another if any of you has a grievance against someone. Forgive as the Lord forgave you." When errors arise, confess truly, and when forgiveness is requested, provide it fully. This cycle of apology and forgiveness develops an atmosphere of grace and understanding.

- **Praying Together:**

Lastly, but definitely not least, add prayer in your conversation. Philippians 4:6-7 (NIV) reminds us of the peace that comes through prayer: "Do not be anxious about anything, but in every situation, by prayer and petition, with thanksgiving, present your requests to God. And the peace of God, which transcends all understanding, will guard your hearts and your minds in Christ Jesus." Praying together not only invites divine guidance into your family but also strengthens your spiritual connection with each other.

Grandparents and Extended Family

As you traverse the thrilling, often trying, terrain of motherhood, the presence and support of grandparents and extended family may be like a compass, guiding you with knowledge, love, and a feeling of continuity. So, let's analyse the importance of these ties and explore how they enhance the fabric of your family's narrative.

A Tapestry of Generations

Imagine your family as a tapestry — a woven masterpiece of varied strands, each adding to the beauty of the whole. In Proverbs 17:6 (NIV), we receive a glimpse of this beauty: "Children's children are a crown to the aged, and parents are the pride of their children." As you step into fatherhood, your kid becomes a part of this living tapestry, linking generations in a manner that is really magnificent.

Wisdom of Experience

Grandparents contribute a treasure wealth of experience and insight. In Job 12:12 (NIV), we're reminded of the knowledge that comes with age: "Is not wisdom found among the aged? Does not long life bring understanding?"

The experiences your parents and in-laws have acquired over the years are like a compass, leading you through the unknown seas of motherhood. Their ideas, opinions, and tales become useful tools as you traverse the complicated terrain of parenting a kid.

Generational Blessings

In Deuteronomy 7:9 (NIV), we see the concept of generational blessings: "Know therefore that the Lord your God is God; he is the faithful God, keeping his covenant of love to a thousand generations of those who love him and keep his commandments." The love and care extended by grandparents lay the foundation for blessings that flow through generations. Your kid receives not simply the affection of their grandparents but also the rich tapestry of family values and customs handed down through the decades.

Shared Traditions and Stories

Grandparents are the custodians of family traditions and history. Psalm 78:4 (NIV) speaks to the importance of passing down stories to the next generation: "We will not hide them from their descendants; we will tell the next generation the praiseworthy deeds of the Lord, his power, and the wonders he has done." The tales of family history, the triumphs, and even the challenges, create a sense of continuity. Embrace the stories your parents and in-laws offer — they're not simply tales of the past but gems that create your child's personality.

Support System

In the journey of motherhood, having a solid support system is vital. Ecclesiastes 4:9-10 (NIV) brilliantly depicts the power gained in unity: "Two are better than one, because they have a good return for their labor: If either of them falls down, one can help the other up." Grandparents and extended family give an extra layer of support. Whether it's extending a helping hand, delivering words of encouragement, or just being there to share the pleasures and trials, their presence makes the parenting experience more bearable and satisfying.

Passing on Faith

The passing on of religion is a holy obligation. In 2 Timothy 1:5 (NIV), we see the impact of a generational faith journey: "I am reminded of your sincere faith, which first lived in your grandmother Lois and in your mother Eunice and, I am persuaded, now lives in you also." Grandparents often play a significant role in shaping a child's spiritual foundation. The prayers, morals, and religion practices they share contribute to the spiritual heritage carried down through generations.

Building Bridges of Love

Your child's connection with their grandparents is a bridge between the past and the future. 1 Corinthians 13:7 (NIV) brilliantly depicts love's eternal nature: "It always protects, always trusts, always hopes, always perseveres." The love exchanged between your kid and their grandparents builds a link that transcends beyond time. It provides a source of comfort, stability, and a basis for good connections throughout their life.

Quality Time and Bonding

The gift of time is one of the most important things grandparents can provide. In Colossians 3:14 (NIV), we're reminded of the significance of love, which links everything together in perfect harmony: "And over all these virtues put on love, which binds them all together in perfect unity." Encourage and encourage meaningful time between your kid and their grandparents. Whether it's shared activities, trips, or simple moments of connection, these encounters generate enduring memories and cement the links of love.

Respecting Boundaries

While the support of extended family is crucial, it's necessary to create appropriate limits. Proverbs 25:17 (NIV) talks to the necessity of moderation: "Seldom set foot in your neighbor's house—too much of you, and they will hate you." Clear communication and mutual respect for limits guarantee that everyone's position is known and appreciated. This transparency leads to a pleasant family dynamic.

Navigating Differences

Differences in parenting techniques or opinions may occur, and that's entirely natural. Proverbs 15:22 (NIV) advises seeking guidance: "Plans fail for lack of counsel, but with many advisers, they succeed." If you find yourself negotiating disputes with grandparents or extended relatives, approach these situations with patience and an open heart. Seek to comprehend one other's opinions, and remember that the shared aim is the well-being and happiness of your kid.

Creating Shared Traditions

While grandparents bring their traditions, consider developing new ones together. Ecclesiastes 3:1 (NIV) beautifully captures the essence of seasons: "There is a time for everything, and a season for every activity under the heavens." Whether it's a yearly family trip, a special holiday tradition, or a monthly gathering, these shared experiences become the building blocks of a unique family identity.

Intergenerational Lessons

Grandparents give essential life lessons. Proverbs 16:31 (NIV) praises the beauty of aging: "Gray hair is a crown of splendor; it is attained in the way of righteousness." The lessons gathered through decades of life experiences become a source of wisdom for your kid. Encourage your youngster to treasure and learn from the wisdom hidden in the tales and guidance of their grandparents.

Resilience and Strength

In times of difficulties, the tenacity and power of extended family show through. Psalm 71:18 (NIV) speaks to passing on God's power and righteousness to the next generation: "Even when I am old and gray, do not forsake me, my God, till I declare your power to the next generation, your mighty acts to all who are to come." The intergenerational support system becomes a testament to the power of love, faith, and resilience.

Celebrating Milestones Together

Milestones in your child's life are occasions for joy. In Romans 12:15 (NIV), we're urged to celebrate with those who rejoice: "Rejoice with those who rejoice; mourn with those who mourn." Invite grandparents and extended family to partake in these wonderful events. Whether it's a birthday, graduation, or a big milestone, these shared celebrations provide a feeling of togetherness and stress the value of family relationships.

Passing Down Traditions

As your kid develops, support the handing down of customs from generation to generation. In Joel 1:3 (NIV), we see the importance of passing on stories to future generations: "Tell it to your children, and let your children tell it to their children, and their children to the next generation." The traditions, values, and stories shared by grandparents become a legacy that continues to shape the identity of your family.

Appreciating Different Roles

Every family member, whether a grandparent, aunt, uncle, or cousin, plays a particular function in your child's life. 1 Corinthians 12:14 (NIV) likens the body of Christ to a body with many parts: "Even so, the body is not made up of one part but of many." Appreciate and cherish the different functions that each family member contributes. Each partnership offers a particular flavor to your child's upbringing.

Building Bridges Between Families

Your child's bond with their extended family is like a bridge connecting various families. Ephesians 4:3 (NIV) stresses keeping unity: "Make every effort to keep the unity of the Spirit through the bond of peace." Foster an atmosphere where families come together, participate in each other's joys and sorrows, and develop bridges that create a feeling of a broader, supportive community.

Inclusion and Diversity

Extended family exposing your kid to a varied assortment of personalities, ethnicities, and experiences. In Revelation 7:9 (NIV), we catch a glimpse of heavenly diversity: "After this, I looked, and there before me was a great multitude that no one could count, from every nation, tribe, people, and language, standing before the throne and before the Lamb." Embrace the richness that diversity brings to your child's life. It broadens their viewpoints, creates acceptance, and encourages a sense of tolerance.

Expressing Gratitude

Finally, express thanks for the role grandparents and extended relatives play in your child's life. 1 Thessalonians 5:18 (NIV) promotes appreciation in all situations: "Give thanks in all circumstances; for this is God's will for you in

Christ Jesus." Let your parents and in-laws know how much you appreciate their love, support, and the wonderful influence they make on your family.

Celebrating Milestones

Celebrating Milestones in your path through parenting. Parenthood is a tapestry woven with innumerable milestones - those beautiful moments that highlight your child's growth and development. Each step, each success, is a cause to rejoice and create lasting memories. So, let's discuss the importance of these milestones, the pleasure they provide, and how they form the building blocks of a wonderful family tale.

A Symphony of Firsts

The early days of fatherhood are a symphony of "firsts" — the first grin, the first walk, the first word. In the book of James 1:17 (NIV), it states, "Every good and perfect gift is from above, coming down from the Father of the heavenly lights, who does not change like shifting shadows." Your kid is a gift, and each milestone offers a glimpse of the unique person they are becoming. Celebrate these firsts with thankfulness, acknowledging the divine beauty in every stage of their journey.

The Importance of Celebration

Celebrating milestones is more than simply a joyous event; it's a method of validating and celebrating your child's progress. Ecclesiastes 3:1 (NIV) refers to the seasons of life: "There is a time for everything, and a season for every activity under the heavens." Each milestone is a landmark in the season of your child's existence. By celebrating, you're not just expressing delight but also reaffirming the value of these occasions.

Creating Lasting Memories

Moments of celebration become treasured memories for both you and your kid. Proverbs 10:7 (NIV) eloquently encapsulates the core of a legacy: "The name of the righteous is used in blessings, but the name of the wicked will rot." When you commemorate milestones, you're engraving good and affirming memories into the fabric of your family narrative. These memories become part of the legacy you're establishing for your kid.

Acknowledging Progress

Every milestone, large or little, is a step forward in your child's growth. Philippians 1:6 (NIV) reassures us of God's work in progress: "Being confident of this, that he who began a good work in you will carry it on to completion until the day of Christ Jesus." Celebrating milestones is a way of acknowledging the progress your child is making – physically, emotionally, and intellectually. It's a reminder that progress is a lovely, continual adventure.

Expressing Love and Affirmation

In Romans 12:10 (NIV), we're urged to respect one another: "Be devoted to one another in love. Honor one another above yourselves." Celebrating milestones is a method of demonstrating love and honor to your kid. It conveys that you perceive and respect their efforts, providing a feeling of affirmation that is vital for their self-esteem and confidence.

Birthdays: A Yearly Celebration of Life

Birthdays are among the most anticipated milestones, and they are definitely a celebration of life. Psalm 139:13-14 (NIV) beautifully reflects on the miracle of life: "For you created my inmost being; you knit me together in my mother's womb. I praise you because I am fearfully and wonderfully made; your works are wonderful, I know that full well." As you celebrate your child's birthday, reflect on the miraculous journey of their life. Consider making it a day not only about presents but about expressing thanks for the unique people they are becoming.

Educational Milestones

As your kid commences on their educational path, celebrate milestones connected to learning. Proverbs 4:7 (NIV) speaks to the value of wisdom: "The beginning of wisdom is this: Get wisdom. Though it cost all you have, get understanding." Whether it's the first day of school, learning to read, or graduating to a higher grade, these moments are opportunities to instill a love for learning and the pursuit of wisdom.

Spiritual Milestones

If your family follows a religion tradition, spiritual milestones are especially meaningful. Proverbs 22:6 (NIV) offers guidance on raising children: "Start children off on the way they should go, and even when they are old they will not turn from it." Celebrate moments such as your child's first prayer, their understanding of spiritual concepts, or their involvement in religious activities. These milestones add to the spiritual foundation you're creating for them.

Social and Emotional Milestones

Your child's social and emotional development is a fertile area for milestones. 1 Thessalonians 5:11 (NIV) supports building each other up: "Therefore encourage one another and build each other up, just as in fact, you are doing." Celebrate occasions when your kid meets a new friend, exhibits empathy, or handles a hard circumstance with fortitude. These milestones contribute to their emotional intelligence and social abilities.

Physical Achievements

From the first crawl to the first successful bike ride, physical milestones are a tribute to your child's improving strength and coordination. 1 Corinthians 6:19-20 (NIV) reminds us of the sanctity of our bodies: "Do you not know that your bodies are temples of the Holy Spirit, who is in you, whom you have received from God? You are not your own; you were bought at a price. Therefore, honor God with your bodies." Celebrate these achievements as a recognition of the incredible gift of a healthy and capable body.

Creative and Artistic Milestones

If your youngster displays an interest in creative activities, acknowledge their artistic successes. Exodus 35:35 (NIV) speaks of God's gifts of craftsmanship: "He has filled them with skill to do all kinds of work as engravers, designers, embroiderers in blue, purple and scarlet yarn and fine linen, and weavers—all of them skilled workers and designers." Whether it's their first drawing, a musical performance, or a crafted masterpiece, these milestones reflect the unique gifts bestowed upon them.

Potty Training and Self-Care

Ah, the adventures of toilet training! It may seem like a modest effort, but it's a critical milestone in your child's road toward independence. In 1 Corinthians 10:31 (NIV), we're reminded to do everything for the glory of God: "So whether you eat or drink or whatever you do, do it all for the glory of God." Celebrate these moments of increased independence and self-care, noting the modest steps that lead to greater autonomy.

Celebrating Effort, Not Just Outcome

It's vital to appreciate the work your kid puts into completing milestones, not simply the reward. Colossians 3:23 (NIV) speaks to the importance of doing everything wholeheartedly: "Whatever you do, work at it with all your heart, as working for the Lord, not for human masters." Whether they succeed or face challenges, recognizing their effort fosters a growth mindset and resilience in the face of setbacks.

Inclusive Celebrations

As you celebrate milestones, consider making them inclusive events. Invite grandparents, extended family, and close friends to join in the excitement. In Romans 12:15 (NIV), we're encouraged to celebrate with those who rejoice: "Rejoice with those who rejoice; mourn with those who mourn." Inclusive celebrations build the feeling of community and support around your kid.

Documenting and Reflecting

Take the time to capture milestones via photographs, films, or diaries. Habakkuk 2:2 (NIV) encourages making visions clear: "Then the Lord replied: 'Write down the revelation and make it plain on tablets so that a herald may run with it.'" Documenting milestones not only preserves the memories but also allows you and your child to reflect on the journey, recognizing growth and progress.

Setting Realistic Expectations

While celebrating milestones, it's crucial to establish reasonable expectations. 1 Corinthians 13:11 (NIV) relates to the process of maturity: "When I was a child, I talked like a child, I thought like a child, I reasoned like a child. When I became a man, I put the ways of childhood behind me." Recognize that each child grows at their own speed, and milestones may differ. Setting reasonable expectations means that celebrations are centred on the particular path of your kid.

Encouraging Future Goals

Milestones are not only about looking back; they're also about looking ahead. Philippians 3:13-14 (NIV) speaks to pressing on toward the goal: "Brothers and sisters, I do not consider myself yet to have taken hold of it. But one thing I do: Forgetting what is behind and straining toward what is ahead, I press on toward the goal to win the prize for which God has called me heavenward in Christ Jesus." Encourage your child to set and pursue future goals, recognizing that each milestone is a stepping stone toward their dreams.

Thanksgiving & Gratitude

In all occasions, show thankfulness and gratitude. 1 Thessalonians 5:16-18 (NIV) encourages a spirit of thanksgiving: "Rejoice always, pray continually, give thanks in all circumstances; for this is God's will for you in Christ Jesus." Recognize the blessings inherent in each milestone and express gratitude for the privilege of witnessing your child's growth.

Reflecting on God's Faithfulness

As you celebrate milestones, reflect on God's faithfulness along the road. Psalm 100:5 (NIV) relates to the lasting nature of God's love: "For the Lord is good and his love endures forever; his faithfulness continues through all generations." Your child's milestones are a monument to God's faithfulness, leading and nourishing them through each season of life.

Chapter 4: Self-Care for Dads

As you begin on this great adventure of parenthood, it's vital to remember that taking care of yourself is not a luxury but a need. Just like the safety warnings on an airline urge you to put on your oxygen mask first before aiding others, practicing self-care empowers you to be the best dad you can be. So, let's discuss what self-care looks like for fathers and how including it into your routine may lead to a better, more meaningful parenting experience.

Understanding Self-Care

Self-care is not selfish; it's an essential element of sustaining your well-being. In 1 Corinthians 6:19-20 (NIV), the Bible reminds us that our bodies are temples of the Holy Spirit: "Do you not know that your bodies are temples of the Holy Spirit, who is in you, whom you have received from God? You are not your own; you were bought at a price. Therefore, honor God with your bodies." Taking care of yourself honors the gift of life that God has entrusted to you.

The New Dad Challenge

Becoming a parent is a tremendous, life-changing event. It's packed with pleasure, love, and an abundance of new duties.

However, these obligations may also lead to disregarding your own needs. In Matthew 11:28-30 (NIV), Jesus offers a comforting invitation: "Come to me, all you who are weary and burdened, and I will give you rest. Take my yoke upon you and learn from me, for I am gentle and humble in heart, and you will find rest for your souls. For my yoke is easy and my burden is light." Embrace the rest that comes from balancing your responsibilities with self-care.

Physical Well-Being

Maintaining your physical health is a cornerstone of self-care. In 1 Corinthians 6:19 (NIV), it's emphasized that our bodies are temples of the Holy Spirit: "Do you not know that your bodies are temples of the Holy Spirit, who is in you, whom you have received from God?" Regular exercise, a balanced diet, and adequate rest are essential components of physical well-being. Even in the hustle of parenting, take opportunities to fuel your body and prioritize its health.

Emotional Resilience

Fatherhood is an emotional journey, and it's appropriate to recognise and share your emotions. Proverbs 14:30 (NIV) reminds us of the effect of a calm heart: "A heart at peace gives life to the body, but envy rots the bones." Take time to indulge in things that offer you pleasure, whether it's following a hobby, spending time with loved ones, or just enjoying a quiet moment of thought. Emotional resilience helps you to manage the difficulties of parenthood with grace.

Rest and Sleep

Sleep is a vital commodity for new parents, and the lack of it may take a toll on physical and emotional well-being. In Psalm 127:2 (NIV), we discover awareness of the significance of rest: "In vain you rise early and stay up late, toiling for food to eat— for he grants sleep to those he loves." While sleep may be difficult in the early days of parenthood, prioritize rest whenever you can. Enlist the help of your partner or family to ensure you receive the sleep you need to rejuvenate.

Healthy Boundaries

Establishing appropriate limits is crucial for your well-being. In Galatians 6:2 (NIV), there's a reminder to bear each other's responsibilities: "Carry each other's burdens, and in this way, you will fulfill the law of Christ." However, it's necessary to identify your boundaries and express them properly. Whether it's distributing duties, saying no when necessary, or requesting help, keeping healthy boundaries ensures that you can complete your commitments without feeling overwhelmed.

Spiritual Nourishment

Nurturing your spiritual well-being is a core part of self-care. In Matthew 4:4 (NIV), Jesus highlights the necessity of spiritual nourishment: "Jesus answered, 'It is written: Man shall not live on bread alone, but on every word that comes from the mouth of God.'" Dedicate time for prayer, meditation, and interacting with spiritual teachings. A solid spiritual basis gives direction, consolation, and perspective in the face of life's trials.

Connection with Others

Fatherhood may often seem alienating, particularly if you're handling the obstacles on your own. In Ecclesiastes 4:9-10 (NIV), there's wisdom in the power of companionship: "Two are better than one because they have a good return for their labor: If either of them falls down, one can help the other up. But pity anyone who falls and has no one to help them up." Cultivate connections with fellow dads, friends, or support groups. Sharing experiences and asking advice develops a feeling of community and support.

Mindful Moments

In the middle of stressful days, carve out moments for mindfulness. In Philippians 4:8 (NIV), there's guidance on focusing our thoughts: "Finally, brothers and sisters, whatever is true, whatever is noble, whatever is right, whatever is pure, whatever is lovely, whatever is admirable—if anything is excellent or praiseworthy—think about such things." Whether it's a few minutes of deep breathing, a walk in nature, or a moment of gratitude, mindful practices contribute to mental well-being.

Quality Time with Your Partner

Maintaining a solid relationship with your spouse is a vital facet of self-care for fathers. In Genesis 2:24 (NIV), there's a profound statement about the unity of marriage: "That is why a man leaves his father and mother and is united to his wife, and they become one flesh." Schedule regular quality time together, whether it's a date night, a heartfelt conversation, or simply enjoying each other's company. A solid relationship gives reciprocal support throughout the path of motherhood.

Seeking Professional Support

If you find yourself battling with the difficulties of parenting, getting professional assistance is a bold and prudent decision. In Proverbs 15:22 (NIV), there's wisdom in seeking advice: "Plans fail for lack of counsel, but with many advisers, they succeed." A counselor or therapist may give direction, teach coping skills, and create a safe environment for you to examine your ideas and emotions.

Hobbies & Passion Pursuits

Maintaining a relationship with your interests and hobbies is a sort of self-care. In Ecclesiastes 3:22 (NIV), there's an acknowledgment of the joy found in one's toil: "So I saw that there is nothing better for a person than to enjoy their work because that is their lot." Whether it's sports, music, reading, or any other pursuit, dedicating time to activities you love rejuvenates your spirit and brings balance to your life.

Gratitude Practices

In all facets of self-care, including gratitude practices may be transformational. In 1 Thessalonians 5:16-18 (NIV), there's a command to rejoice, pray, and give thanks: "Rejoice always, pray continually, give thanks in all circumstances; for this is God's will for you in Christ Jesus." Cultivate a practise of expressing thankfulness for the benefits in your life. It redirects your emphasis toward the positive and promotes an attitude of abundance.

Balancing Responsibilities

Self-care is about finding equilibrium in the middle of obligations. In Colossians 3:23 (NIV), there's guidance on doing everything wholeheartedly: "Whatever you do, work at it with all your heart, as working for the Lord, not for human masters." Approach your responsibilities with dedication, but remember that taking care of yourself is not a distraction from your duties; it enhances your ability to fulfill them with love and commitment.

Setting Realistic Expectations

Lastly, it's vital to establish reasonable expectations for yourself. In Philippians 4:13 (NIV), there's a reminder of God's power inside us: "I can do all this through him who gives me strength." Recognize that you are not expected to be flawless, and it's alright to ask for assistance. Setting realistic expectations helps you to approach parenting with grace and humility.

Finding Time for Yourself

Today, let's dig into a subject that could seem elusive amid the rush of new parenting - "Finding Time for Yourself." I understand it; with the diaper changes, restless nights, and the continuous baby talk, the thought of carving out time for yourself might seem like a faraway dream. But believe me, it's not just a luxury; it's a need. So, let's discuss why it's vital, how to make it happen, and how one tiny act of self-care can make a world of difference.

- **The New Dad Hustle:**

You've definitely heard the expression, "It takes a village to raise a child." Well, it also requires a little of "me time" to keep you sane in the middle of the parent rush. In Mark 6:31 (NIV), Jesus acknowledges the necessity for relaxation: "Then, because so many people were coming and going that they did not even have a chance to eat, he said to them, 'Come with me by yourselves to a quiet place and get some rest.'" Even Jesus realised the value of stepping away for a break.

- **Why Finding Time for Yourself Matters:**

Okay, let's get real. As a parent, you're juggling a lot — the baby's requirements, work, domestic tasks, and maybe attempting to catch some z's in between. But here's the deal: taking time for yourself isn't a selfish act; it's a sanity-saving manoeuvre. In Galatians 6:9 (NIV), there's a nugget of wisdom about not giving up: "Let us not become weary in doing good, for at the proper time, we will reap a harvest if we do not give up." Taking time for yourself is a way of preventing burnout, ensuring you can keep doing the good stuff without wearing yourself out.

- **Quality above Quantity:**

Alright, I know what you're thinking - "Time for myself? Where am I going to find that?" I hear you. You don't need an entire day at the spa (though that does sound lovely). Sometimes, it's about quality over quantity. In Matthew 6:6 (NIV), Jesus talks about finding a quiet place: "But when you pray, go into your room, close the door and pray to your Father, who is unseen. Then your Father, who sees what is done in secret, will reward you." Your quiet place might not be a literal room, but finding those small moments for yourself can be just as rewarding.

- **How to Make It Happen:**

Now, let's get practical. How on earth can you find time for oneself when the baby's needs seem never-ending? It's all about being thoughtful and a little imaginative. Remember, it's not about the amount of time; it's about the quality.

- **Early Morning Moments:**

I know, you're probably not getting much sleep as it is. But try getting up just a touch early before the rest of the house stirs. In Psalm 5:3 (NIV), there's a wonderful mention of the morning: "In the morning, Lord, you hear my voice; in the morning, I lay my requests before you and wait expectantly." Use these peaceful hours for prayer, thought, or just drinking a cup of coffee in solitude.

- **Delegate and Share the Load:**

You're not a superhero (well, not all the time). Don't hesitate to distribute duties or share responsibility with your companion. Proverbs 15:22 (NIV) reminds us of the value of seeking advice: "Plans fail for lack of counsel, but with many advisers, they succeed." Discuss your need for a little of personal time, then work together to make it happen.

- **Lunch Break retreat:**

If you're working outside the house, try utilising your lunch break as a short retreat. Whether it's a brief stroll, a quiet location to read, or even simply shutting your eyes for a few minutes, these tiny pauses may be revitalising.

- **Naptime Ninja Moves:**

When the tiny one takes a nap, that's your golden chance. In Isaiah 30:15 (NIV), there's a mention to the rest found in stillness and trust: "In repentance and rest is your salvation, in quietness and trust is your strength." Use this time to replenish your batteries - whether it's a power nap, reading a book, or doing something you like.

- **Evening Wind-Down:**

After the baby is down for the night, resist the impulse to get right into housework. Take a minute for yourself. In Psalm 119:147 (NIV), there's a mention of reflecting on God's promises in the evening: "I rise before dawn and cry for help; I have put my hope in your word." It doesn't have to be a spiritual exercise; it may be anything that provides you comfort.

- **Benefits of Finding Time for Yourself:**

Okay, let's speak about the nice things. What happens when you truly manage to locate those precious minutes for yourself? Well, my buddy, it's a game-changer.

- **Rejuvenation for Dad Mode:**

Taking time for yourself is like pushing the reset button on your dad mode. In Isaiah 40:31 (NIV), there's a beautiful promise for those who hope in the Lord: "But those who hope in the Lord will renew their strength. They will soar on wings like eagles; they will run and not grow weary, they will walk and not be faint." Consider your "me time" as a form of hope and renewal.

- **Increased Patience and Presence:**

When you've taken a minute to recharge, you bring a new degree of patience and presence to the parenting game. In Colossians 3:12 (NIV), there's a command to cover ourselves with compassion and patience: "Therefore, as God's chosen people, holy and dearly loved, clothe yourselves with compassion, kindness, humility, gentleness, and patience." Your "me time" is like putting on the garment of patience.

- **Enhanced Mental Well-Being:**

Your mental well-being counts just as much as your physical health. In Philippians 4:8 (NIV), there's guidance on focusing our thoughts: "Finally, brothers and sisters, whatever is true, whatever is noble, whatever is right, whatever is pure, whatever is lovely, whatever is admirable—if anything is excellent or praiseworthy—think about such things." Your moments of solitude can be a sanctuary for positive thoughts.

- **Strengthened Relationships:**

Believe it or not, spending time for yourself may help boost your relationships. When you're in a healthy mental and emotional place, your relationships with your spouse and infant become more pleasant. In 1 Corinthians 16:14 (NIV), there's a simple but powerful directive: "Do everything in love." Your "me time" adds to a loving and happy household.

- **Modeling Self-Care for Your kid:**

Lastly, by prioritizing your well-being, you're modeling a crucial life skill for your kid. In Proverbs 22:6 (NIV), there's counsel on bringing up a child: "Start children off on the way they should go, and even when they are old, they will not turn from it." Show them that self-care is not selfish but an essential element of a healthy, balanced existence.

- **Embrace the Journey:**

In the crazy and magnificent adventure of parenthood, making time for yourself is not a luxury; it's a lifeline. So, my fellow dad, accept the adventure. It's good to seek those moments of quiet among the diapers and baby smiles. Your well-being matters, and it's not a solo mission. Lean on your support system, be intentional about your "me time," and savor those moments of peace. May your fatherhood adventure be filled with joy, love, and a few quiet moments just for you. You've got this!

Staying Healthy and Fit

Today, let's discuss about an issue that's frequently ignored in the rush of fatherhood — "Staying Healthy and Fit." Now, I get it; with the near birth of your young one, you may be wondering how on earth you'll fit in a workout when sleep is becoming a valuable commodity. But believe me, keeping your health and fitness is not only about looking beautiful; it's about equipping yourself to be the greatest parent you can be. So, let's discuss why it matters, how to make it happen, and how the good book has some wisdom to aid you on this trip.

- **The Dad Bod Dilemma:**

You've certainly heard of the "dad bod" — that relaxed figure that may creep up on new dads. Between restless nights and the countless newborn tasks, keeping fit could be the last thing on your mind. But here's the deal: taking care of your health is not only for you; it's for your young one too. In 1 Corinthians 6:19-20 (NIV), there's a reminder that your body is a temple of the Holy Spirit: "Do you not know that your bodies are temples of the Holy Spirit, who is in you, whom you have received from God? You are not your own; you were purchased at a price. Therefore, worship God with your body." Taking care of your body acknowledges the gift of life bestowed to you.

Why Staying Healthy Matters:
Alright, let's get real. Why should being healthy and active be a priority in the hectic world of diapers and baby bottles?

- **Energy for Dad Duty:**

Fatherhood is like a marathon. You need stamina, endurance, and a bit of sprinting now and then. Staying healthy helps you have the energy to accomplish those parenting chores with enthusiasm. In Isaiah 40:31 (NIV), there's a great promise for those who trust in the Lord: "But those who hope in the Lord will replenish their strength. They will soar on wings like eagles; they will run and not be tired, they will walk and not be faint." Your health journey is like recharging your power for the dad marathon.

- **Setting a Healthy Example:**

Kids are sponges; they pick up everything, including your actions. By prioritizing your health, you're setting a good example for your little one. In Proverbs 22:6 (NIV), there's instruction on bringing up a child: "Start children off on the way they should go, and even when they are old, they will not turn from it." Show them the route to a healthy and active life.

- **Stress Management:**

Fatherhood comes with its fair share of stress. Staying active is a terrific stress buster. In Philippians 4:6-7 (NIV), there's counsel on coping with anxiety: "Do not be worried about anything, but in every circumstance, by prayer and supplication, with thanksgiving, submit your requests to God. And the peace of God, which surpasses all understanding, will protect your hearts and your thoughts in Christ Jesus." Consider exercise as a type of prayer for a quiet heart.

- **Quality Time with Your Little One:**

Being fit helps you to completely participate in those precious times with your kid. Whether it's playing, going for a stroll, or just carrying them around, your physical health adds to the quality of time spent together. In Ecclesiastes 3:1 (NIV), there's a realisation of the seasons of life: "There is a time for everything, and a season for every activity under the heavens." Embrace the season of busy, lively parenting.

- **Making It Happen - Practical Tips:**

Now that we've established why it's vital, let's talk about how to make remaining healthy and fit a reality in the dad world.

- **Short Bursts of Activity:**

You may not have the luxury of extensive gym sessions, and that's alright. Break it down into small, focused spurts. In 1

Timothy 4:8 (NIV), there's awareness of the benefit of physical exercise: "For physical training is of some value, but godliness has value for all things, holding promise for both the present life and the life to come." Even small spurts of action carry worth.

- **Incorporate Baby into Workouts:**

Get inventive! Use your baby as a weight during exercises. They could find it entertaining, and you get a tiny exercise. It's a win-win. In Deuteronomy 6:5 (NIV), there's a command to love God with all your might: "Love the Lord your God with all your heart and with all your soul and with all your strength." Incorporating exercise into your routine is a means of honouring God with your power.

- **Prioritize Sleep:**

I know, I know. Sleep is already in limited supply. But hear me out. In Psalm 127:2 (NIV), there's an awareness of the futility of toiling without rest: "In vain you rise early and stay up late, toiling for food to eat— for he grants sleep to those he loves." Prioritizing sleep benefits to your overall health and fitness.

- **Involve Your Partner:**

Staying healthy is a team effort. Get your partner engaged! Whether it's taking turns for solitary exercises or participating in physical activities together, the mutual support is important. In Ecclesiastes 4:9-10 (NIV), there's wisdom in the strength of companionship: "Two are better than one because they have a good return for their labor."

- **Nutrition Matters:**

Exercise alone won't cut it. Pay attention to what you're nourishing your body with. In 1 Corinthians 10:31 (NIV), there's counsel on doing everything for the glory of God: "So whether you eat or drink or whatever you do, do it all for the glory of God." Choose healthful meals that appreciate your body.

- **Maintaining Consistency - The Dad Edition:**

Consistency is crucial, but let's be honest - it's not always easy when dad responsibilities are calling. So, how can you remain constant in your health and fitness journey?

- **Set Realistic Goals:**

Be realistic about what you can accomplish in your present season of life. In Philippians 4:13 (NIV), there's a reminder of God's power inside us: "I can do all this through him who gives me strength." Set objectives that match with your existing duties.

- **Find Accountability:**

Whether it's a gym companion, your spouse, or a fitness app, find something that keeps you accountable. In Proverbs 27:17 (NIV), there's wisdom in the sharpening impact of one person on another: "As iron sharpens iron, so one person sharpens another."

- **Embrace the Dad Bod Days:**

There will be days when the dad responsibilities take priority. Embrace those days. In Ecclesiastes 3:1-2 (NIV), there's wisdom in the seasons of life: "There is a time for everything, and a season for every activity under the heavens: a time to be born and a time to die." Accept the ebb and flow of your fitness journey.

- **Celebrate Small Wins:**

Maybe you didn't get in a complete exercise, but you managed a brief stretch. Celebrate it! In Zephaniah 3:17 (NIV), there's a magnificent vision of God rejoicing over us: "The Lord your God is with you, the Mighty Warrior who rescues. He will take great interest in you; in his love, he will no longer reprimand you, but will rejoice over you with song." Rejoice in your minor successes.

- **Benefits Beyond the Physical:**

Staying healthy and active isn't only about pumping iron or dropping pounds. The advantages extend beyond the physical world.

- **Mental Clarity:**

Regular exercise increases mental clarity and attention. In Romans 12:2 (NIV), there's a command to refresh our minds: "Do not conform to the pattern of this world but be transformed by the renewing of your mind." Exercise is a means of rejuvenating your thoughts.

- **Emotional Well-Being:**

Physical exercise releases endorphins, those feel-good chemicals. In Proverbs 17:22 (NIV), there's a realisation of the significance of a joyful heart: "A cheerful heart is good medicine, but a crushed spirit dries up the bones." Exercise is like medication for your heart.

- **Improved Sleep:**

Regular exercise adds to greater sleep quality. In Psalm 4:8 (NIV), there's a magnificent depiction of finding calm in God's safety: "In peace, I will lie down and sleep, for you alone, Lord, make me dwell in safety."

- **Enhanced Confidence:**

Taking care of your health enhances your confidence. In 1 Corinthians 10:31 (NIV), there's counsel on doing everything for the glory of God: "So whether you eat or drink or whatever you do, do it all for the glory of God." Your health journey is an act of worshipping God via self-care.

- **Embrace the Journey, Dad:**

So, there you have it, prospective dad! Staying healthy and active isn't an added responsibility; it's a gift to yourself and your family. It's about respecting the temple God handed to you, ensuring you have the energy to accept the pleasures and trials of parenting. As you begin on this road, remember the words of 3 John 1:2 (NIV): "Dear friend, I pray that you may enjoy good health and that all may go well with you, even as your soul is getting along well." May your road to health and fitness be one of pleasure, consistency, and the odd dad bod day. You've got this!

Mental Well-being

Today, let's dig into a subject that sometimes takes a second seat in the flurry of approaching parenthood — "Mental Well-being." Trust me, I understand it. With the excitement, the preparations, and maybe a touch of worry, it's easy for your mental well-being to be overshadowed. But here's the thing: taking care of your mind is just as vital as setting up the crib or buying the appropriate stroller. So, let's discuss why it important, how to maintain your mental well-being, and how the good book gives some insight to assist you through this portion of the dad journey.

- **The Silent fight:**

In the middle of baby showers and nursery decorating, mental well-being frequently becomes the silent fight. The reality is, transitioning to parenthood may be stressful. From restless nights to the weight of new duties, it's natural to experience a combination of emotions. In Psalm 34:17-18 (NIV), there's a consoling promise for those who cry out: "The righteous cry out, and the Lord hears them; he saves them from all their worries. The Lord is near to the brokenhearted and rescues those who are crushed in spirit." Your screams, whether vocal or quiet, are heard.

Why Mental Well-being Matters:

Alright, let's get real. Why should mental well-being be a concern when you walk into the domain of fatherhood?

- **Being Present for Your Family:**

Your mental well-being immediately influences your capacity to be there for your spouse and your little one. In Colossians 3:2 (NIV), there's counsel on placing our thoughts on things above: "Set your minds on things above, not on earthly things." Nurturing your mental well-being helps you to concentrate on the greater calling of parenthood.

- **Building Resilience:**

Fatherhood is a journey of resilience. In James 1:2-4 (NIV), there's understanding of the refining process of difficulties: "Consider it pure pleasure, dear brothers and sisters, whenever you meet trials of various sorts because you know that the testing of your faith creates perseverance. Let persistence finish its job so that you may be mature and complete, without wanting anything." Your mental well-being is crucial to handling the adversities with pleasure and tenacity.

- **Setting a Positive Example:**

Your young one is observing and learning from you. By prioritizing your mental well-being, you're setting a healthy example for kids. In Philippians 4:8 (NIV), there's direction on concentrating our thoughts: "Finally, brothers and sisters, whatever is true, whatever is noble, whatever is right, whatever is pure, whatever is lovely, whatever is admirable—if anything is excellent or praiseworthy—think about such things." Your mental patterns effect the ambiance of your house.

- **Navigating difficulties:**

Fatherhood comes with its own difficulties. Your mental well-being helps you to manage these problems with grace and resilience. In 2 Corinthians 12:9 (NIV), there's a realisation of God's abundant grace in our weakness: "But he replied to me, 'My grace is sufficient for you, because my power is made perfect in weakness.' Therefore, I will boast all the more cheerfully about my weaknesses, so that Christ's strength may rest on me." Embracing your vulnerability is a means to strength.

Nurturing Your Mental Well-being:
Now that we understand why it matters, let's examine practical strategies to nourish your mental well-being as you begin on this new chapter.

- **Open Communication:**

Share your opinions and emotions with your spouse. In Proverbs 15:22 (NIV), there's value in seeking guidance: "Plans fail for lack of counsel, but with many advisers, they succeed." Your companion is a crucial guide throughout your adventure.

- **Seek help:**

Don't hesitate to seek help from friends, family, or even professional counselors. In Ecclesiastes 4:9-10 (NIV), there's wisdom in the strength of companionship: "Two are better than one because they have a good return for their labor: If either of them falls down, one can help the other up." You don't have to tackle the problems alone.

- **Set Realistic Expectations:**

Fatherhood comes with a learning curve. Set reasonable expectations for yourself. In Philippians 4:13 (NIV), there's a reminder of God's power inside us: "I can do all this through him who gives me strength." You are not supposed to have it all figured out.

- **Take Breaks:**

It's good to take breaks when required. In Mark 6:31 (NIV), there's a realisation of the necessity for rest: "Then, because so many people were coming and going that they did not even have a chance to eat, he said to them, 'Come with me by yourselves to a quiet place and get some rest.'" Rest is not a sign of weakness but a necessary for strength.

- **Practice Mindfulness:**

Engage in mindfulness techniques to remain present in the moment. In Psalm 46:10 (NIV), there's a call to be quiet and know God: "He says, 'Be still, and know that I am God; I will be exalted among the nations, I will be exalted in the earth.'" Being present in the moment develops a feeling of tranquilly.

- **Overcoming Mental challenges:**

If you find yourself suffering mental challenges, realise that you're not alone. It's alright to seek out for assistance. In Psalm 34:18 (NIV), there's a promise for people who are brokenhearted: "The Lord is close to the brokenhearted and saves those who are crushed in spirit." Here are some extra steps:

- **Professional aid:**

If required, don't hesitate to seek professional aid. In Proverbs 12:15 (NIV), there's wisdom in seeking guidance:

"The way of fools seems right to them, but the wise listen to advice." Seeking expert counsel is a sensible approach.

- **Self-Compassion:**

Practice self-compassion on your path. In Ephesians 4:32 (NIV), there's instruction on being kind and compassionate: "Be kind and compassionate to one another, forgiving each other, just as in Christ God forgave you." Extend that warmth and compassion to yourself.

- **Connect with Other parents:**

Share your experiences with other parents. In Galatians 6:2 (NIV), there's a call to bear each other's burdens: "Carry each other's burdens, and in this way, you will fulfill the law of Christ." You're not alone on this path.

- **Prayer and Meditation:**

Engage in prayer and meditation to find consolation. In Philippians 4:6-7 (NIV), there's counsel on coping with anxiety: "Do not be worried about anything, but in every circumstance, by prayer and supplication, with thanksgiving, submit your requests to God. And the peace of God, which surpasses all understanding, will protect your hearts and your thoughts in Christ Jesus." Prayer is a great technique for seeking calm.

- **The Power of Perspective:**

In the face of problems, remember the power of perspective. In Romans 8:28 (NIV), there's a promise for people who love God: "And we know that in all things, God works for the good of those who love him, who have been called according to his purpose." Even despite the trials of parenting, there is a bigger purpose at play.

- **Embrace the Journey, Dad:**

So, my soon-to-be dad buddy, when you move into the world of parenthood, remember that nourishing your mental well-being is not a luxury but a must. It's a journey of perseverance, self-discovery, and accepting the full gamut of emotions that come with becoming a parent. Lean on the support around you, seek assistance when required, and realise that your mental well-being matters significantly. May your path into parenthood be blessed with serenity, joy, and an abundance of love. You've got this!

Hobbies and Personal Time

Today, let's discuss about something that may seem like a distant memory after the baby comes — "Hobbies and Personal Time." Now, I understand it. The concept of personal time could seem like a luxury when you're preparing to enter into the world of diaper changes and late-night feedings. But here's the scoop: keeping your interests and finding a piece of personal time isn't simply a nice-to-have; it's a necessary for your well-being. So, let's discuss why it matters, how to carve out that precious time, and sure, we'll pour in some advice from the good book to aid you on your trip.

The Lost Art of Me-Time

As you stand on the brink of parenthood, it's tempting to envisage a life occupied with baby bottles and bedtime tales. Amidst the delightful pandemonium, your interests and personal time could take a backseat. But here's a reality that may surprise you — hanging onto a portion of yourself, your interests, and your personal time isn't selfish. It's an investment in your own happiness, which, in turn, leads to a more meaningful parenting journey.

Why Hobbies and Personal Time Matter:

Alright, let's get real. Why should you create room for your interests and personal time, even amid the flurry of imminent parent duties?

- **Maintaining Identity:**

Becoming a parent is a big adjustment, but it doesn't erase who you are. In 1 Corinthians 15:58 (NIV), there's a command to stay steady and let nothing shake you: "Therefore, my dear brothers and sisters, stand strong. Let nothing move you. Always commit oneself totally to the work of the Lord because you know that your labor in the Lord is not in vain." Your identity is a wonderful mosaic of roles, and sustaining interests is a way to acknowledge that.

- **Recharging Your Batteries:**

Fatherhood is like a marathon, and every marathon runner has to refuel. In Matthew 11:28-30 (NIV), there's an invitation to find rest in Jesus: "Come to me, all you who are tired and burdened, and I will give you rest. Take my yoke upon you and learn from me, because I am gentle and humble in heart, and you will find rest for your souls." Your activities might be a source of such rest.

- **Setting an Example for Your Child:**

Your tiny one is observing and learning from you. By prioritizing your interests, you're providing an example of balance and self-care. In Proverbs 22:6 (NIV), there's instruction on bringing up a child: "Start children off on the way they should go, and even when they are old, they will not turn from it." Show children the significance of a well-rounded existence.

- **Strengthening Relationships:**

Carving out personal time doesn't imply forsaking your family. In Ecclesiastes 3:1 (NIV), there's a realisation of the seasons of life: "There is a time for everything, and a season for every activity under the heavens." Balancing personal time with family time enhances both.

Carving Out Personal Time - Practical Tips:
Now that we've established why it important, let's talk about how to really make it happen. Trust me, it's doable, even in the crazy but lovely world of imminent parenthood.

- **Schedule It In:**

Yes, arrange personal time as you would a doctor's visit. In Psalm 90:12 (NIV), there's an acknowledgment of the worth of time: "Teach us to number our days, that we may gain a heart of wisdom." Your time is precious, so be deliberate about it.

- **Involve Your Partner:**

Teamwork makes the dream work, right? In Ecclesiastes 4:9-10 (NIV), there's wisdom in the strength of companionship: "Two are better than one because they have a good return for their labor: If either of them falls down, one can help the other up." Share tasks and provide room for each other's personal time.

- **Embrace Short Bursts:**

Maybe extended lengths of personal time are hard to come by. That's alright! Embrace brief spurts of me-time. In 1 Thessalonians 5:16-18 (NIV), there's counsel to "rejoice always, pray continually, give thanks in all circumstances." Even little periods of alone leisure may be times of bliss.

- **Combine Hobbies with Dad Duties:**

Get inventive! Can your interest mesh with parental duties? If you like reading, maybe it's storytime for both you and the baby. In Colossians 3:23 (NIV), there's a reminder to accomplish everything with your entire heart: "Whatever you do, work at it with all your heart, as working for the Lord, not for human masters." Including your hobbies with parent responsibilities is working with your entire heart.

Why Hobbies Are Important for Dads:

Now, let's go a little more into why hobbies especially are vital for parents.

- **Stress Relief:**

Fatherhood, as lovely as it is, comes with its share of stress. Hobbies are a fantastic stress reliever. In Philippians 4:6-7 (NIV), there's counsel on coping with anxiety: "Do not be worried about anything, but in every circumstance, by prayer and supplication, with thanksgiving, submit your requests to God. And the peace of God, which surpasses all understanding, will protect your hearts and your thoughts in Christ Jesus."

- **Fulfillment Outside of Roles:**

While being a dad is a crucial and great job, it's not your sole one. Hobbies bring satisfaction outside of your parenthood obligations. In Galatians 6:4 (NIV), there's a call to test your own activities: "Each one should examine their own deeds. Then people may take satisfaction in themselves alone, without comparing themselves to someone else."

- **Boosting Creativity:**

Whether it's carpentry, painting, or writing, hobbies may improve your creativity. In Genesis 1:27 (NIV), there's a reminder that we are formed in the image of a creative God: "So God created mankind in his own image, in the image of God he created them; male and female he created them." Embrace and express the creativity inside you.

- **Building a Sense of success:**

Completing a carpentry project or completing a chapter in a book offers you a sense of success. In 1 Corinthians 15:58 (NIV), there's a command to stay steady and let nothing shake you: "Therefore, my dear brothers and sisters, stand strong. Let nothing move you. Always commit oneself totally to the work of the Lord because you know that your labor in the Lord is not in vain." Your pursuits, even hobbies, have worth.

- **Navigating the Guilt:**

Now, let's confront the elephant in the room — guilt. It's natural for parents to feel bad about spending personal time. In Mark 6:31 (NIV), there's a realisation of the necessity for rest: "Then, because so many people were coming and going that they did not even have a chance to eat, he said to them, 'Come with me by yourselves to a quiet place and get some rest.'" Rest is not a luxury; it's a need. Release the guilt and appreciate the rest.

- **Embrace the Journey, Dad:**

As you begin on this journey called parenting, remember that keeping your interests and finding personal time isn't a selfish act. It's a chance to be true to yourself, replenish your batteries, and set a great example for your little one. In Philippians 4:13 (NIV), there's a reminder of God's power inside us: "I can do all this through him who gives me strength." You've got this, dad! So, go ahead, take up that instrument, paint that canvas, or just enjoy a peaceful time with a nice book. Your well-being is a vital part of this fantastic journey into parenthood.

Seeking Support

The notion of seeking help may seem basic, but let's deconstruct why it's necessary, how to go about it, and yes, we'll weave in some advice from the good book to aid you on your path.

The Myth of Lone Fatherhood

As you stand on the threshold of dad life, it's tempting to fall into the myth of lone fatherhood — the concept that you should have all the answers and bear all the obligations alone. But here's the truth: asking help is not a sign of weakness; it's a monument to your knowledge and strength. No guy is an island, particularly when it comes to navigating the exhilarating but treacherous seas of parenthood.

Why Seeking Support Matters:
Alright, let's be serious about why seeking help is a game-changer as you move into the dad role:

- **Sharing the Load:**

In Ecclesiastes 4:9 (NIV), there's wisdom in the strength of companionship: "Two are better than one because they have a good return for their labor: If either of them falls down, one can help the other up." Sharing the weight with others lightens your burden and enhances the trip.

- **Learning from Experience:**

Seeking help involves tapping into the collective knowledge of people who've travelled this route before. In Proverbs 19:20 (NIV), there's advise on listening to advice: "Listen to advice and accept discipline, and at the end, you will be counted among the wise." Learning from the experiences of others is a good decision.

- **Emotional Well-being:**

Fatherhood is an emotional rollercoaster. In Galatians 6:2 (NIV), there's a call to bear each other's burdens: "Carry each other's burdens, and in this way, you will fulfill the law of Christ." Sharing your emotional problems with others is a means of fulfilling this obligation.

- **Building a Support System:**

Your support system is like a safety net. In Proverbs 24:6 (NIV), there's wisdom in having a plurality of counselors: "Surely you need guidance to wage war, and victory is won through many advisers." Building a support system prepares you for the difficulties and successes of parenting.

Who Can Be Your Support:

Now, let's speak about who can be part of your support staff. It's not a one-size-fits-all issue, and that's completely good. Your support staff could include:

- **Your Partner:**

Your spouse is your key colleague in this adventure. In Genesis 2:24 (NIV), there's a realisation of the oneness in marriage: "That is why a man leaves his father and mother and is united to his wife, and they become one flesh." Your togetherness with your mate is a strong foundation.

- **Friends:**

True friends are like treasures. In Proverbs 18:24 (NIV), there's wisdom in the importance of faithful friends: "One who has unreliable friends soon comes to ruin, but there is a friend who sticks closer than a brother." Identify those buddies that keep close.

- **Relatives Members:**

Family, whether parents, siblings, or extended relatives, may give vital support. In Ephesians 6:2 (NIV), there's a reminder to respect your parents: "Honor your father and mother—which is the first commandment with a promise." Seeking help from family respects this commandment.

- **Mentors or Experienced fathers:**

If you have mentors or experienced fathers in your group, draw on their knowledge. In Proverbs 13:20 (NIV), there's counsel on travelling with the wise: "Walk with the wise and become wise, for a companion of fools suffers harm." Surround yourself with people who can offer insight.

How to Seek Support:

Now, let's investigate how to really go about getting assistance in your dad journey:

- **Initiate Honest Conversations:**

In James 5:16 (NIV), there's a call to confess and pray for each other: "Therefore confess your faults to each other and pray for each other so that you may be healed. The prayer of a decent person is strong and effective." Initiate honest talks with your support staff, discussing your pleasures and problems.

- **Be Open to guidance:**

In Proverbs 12:15 (NIV), there's wisdom in seeking guidance: "The way of fools seems right to them, but the wise listen to advice." Be receptive to advise from people who've travelled the dad route before you.

- **Join Dad Groups or courses:**

Seek out dad groups or parenting courses in your town. In Proverbs 27:17 (NIV), there's understanding of the influence of iron sharpening iron: "As iron sharpens iron, so one person sharpens another." Surround yourself with other fathers who can sharpen and support you.

- **Utilize Online Communities:**

In this digital era, online communities may be beneficial. In Ecclesiastes 4:12 (NIV), there's wisdom in a string of three strands not soon broken: "Though one may be overcome, two may protect themselves. A string of three strands is not rapidly broken." Online communities provide an additional strand to your support chord.

- **Navigating Pride and Independence:**

Now, let's address a possible stumbling block — pride. It's typical to desire to be the self-sufficient, do-it-all parent. In Proverbs 16:18 (NIV), there's a warning regarding pride: "Pride goes before destruction, a haughty spirit before a fall." Recognize that requesting help is not a show of weakness but of humility and power.

- **How God Supports Us:**

In your desire for support, take solace in the idea that God is the greatest supporter. In Psalm 55:22 (NIV), there's an invitation to lay your troubles on the Lord: "Cast your cares on the Lord and he will sustain you; he will never let the righteous be shaken." God is a solid anchor amid the storms of life, especially the tornado of parenthood.

- **Embrace the Journey, Dad:**

As you embark into the thrilling, often baffling realm of parenthood, remember that seeking help is not a sign of inferiority but an assertion of wisdom. Your path is richer when you allow people to walk beside you. In Proverbs 15:22 (NIV), there's value in seeking guidance: "Plans fail for lack of counsel, but with many advisers, they succeed." May your path be blessed with good guidance, shared hardships, and the strength that comes from the company of supporting hearts. You've got this, dad!

Chapter 5: Looking Ahead

Today, let's have a heart-to-heart about a subject that may not be at the forefront of your thoughts as you anxiously anticipate the birth of your little one — "Looking Ahead." I realise the current moment is both exhilarating and a touch nerve-wracking, but taking a minute to peek into the future may be tremendously meaningful. So, let's discuss why it's vital, what to expect, and, of course, let's throw in some timeless advice from the good book to aid you on your trip.

- **The Adventure of Anticipation:**

As you stand on the edge of parenthood, it's tempting to get captivated by the immediacy of baby showers, nursery preparations, and the imminent delivery day. However, taking a quick stop to gaze forward is like glimpsing into a treasure box of moments waiting to unfold. It's about enjoying the adventure of anticipation, understanding that this is only the beginning of a lifetime of priceless milestones.

- **Why Looking Ahead Matters:**

Alright, let's look into why casting your sight into the future is not only a frivolous thought but a practical and joyful endeavor:

- **Setting Goals and Intentions:**

In Philippians 3:14 (NIV), there's a call to push on toward the goal: "I press on toward the goal to win the prize for which God has called me heavenward in Christ Jesus." As a parent, defining goals and aspirations for your family gives a blueprint for the lovely adventure ahead.

- **Building Traditions:**

Anticipation helps you to anticipate the traditions you wish to develop with your expanding family. In Proverbs 22:6 (NIV), there's wisdom in bringing up a kid in the way they should walk: "Start children off on the way they should go, and even when they are old, they will not turn from it." Your conscious deeds now create the traditions of tomorrow.

- **Planning for problems:**

Looking forward isn't only about picturing the delights; it's also about planning for problems. In James 1:2-4 (NIV), there's understanding of the refining process of difficulties: "Consider it pure pleasure, dear brothers and sisters, whenever you meet trials of various sorts because you know that the testing of your faith creates perseverance. Let persistence finish its job so that you may be mature and complete, without wanting anything." Anticipating problems with a strong attitude is part of the process.

- **Savoring daily Moments:**

Anticipation pushes you to cherish the daily moments. In Ecclesiastes 3:1 (NIV), there's a realisation of the seasons of life: "There is a time for everything, and a season for every activity under the heavens." Each season of parenting brings unique experiences, and looking forward helps you treasure them.

What to Anticipate:

Now, let's discuss what lies on the horizon as you step into the domain of parenthood. Consider these peeks into the future:

- **First Steps and Words:**

Picture the overwhelming thrill of seeing your young one take their first steps or speak their first words. In Psalm 37:23 (NIV), there's a reminder that the Lord delights in the path of the one whose steps are ordered: "The Lord makes firm the steps of the one who delights in him."

- **School Days and Discoveries:**

Anticipate the thrill of school days, when your youngster embarks on a journey of learning and self-discovery. In Proverbs 1:5 (NIV), there's a call to let the wise listen and add to their learning: "Let the wise listen and add to their learning, and let the discerning get guidance."

- **Adventures and experiences:**

Envision the adventures and experiences you'll have as a family. In Joshua 1:9 (NIV), there's an exhortation to be strong and brave in the face of new territories: "Have I not instructed you? Be powerful and bold. Do not be frightened; do not be discouraged, because the Lord your God will be with you wherever you go."

- **Teenage Years and freedom:**

Anticipate the teenage years, as your kid starts to stretch their wings and negotiate the route to freedom. In Proverbs 3:5-6 (NIV), there's wisdom in relying in the Lord's guidance: "Trust in the Lord with all your heart and lean not on your own understanding; in all your ways submit to him, and he will make your paths straight."

Cultivating a Future-Focused Mindset:
Now, let's discuss how to create a future-focused attitude as you embrace the experiences that lie ahead:

- **Set Realistic Goals:**

In 1 Corinthians 9:24 (NIV), there's a call to run the race in such a manner as to win the prize: "Do you not know that in a race all the runners run, but only one gets the prize? Run in such a manner as to grab the reward." Set reasonable objectives for your family, keeping the ultimate reward of a thriving, loving household in mind.

- **Prioritize Quality Time:**

In Psalm 90:12 (NIV), there's an awareness of the worth of time: "Teach us to number our days, that we may gain a heart of wisdom." Prioritize meaningful time with your family, realising the transient nature of moments.

- **Adaptability and Flexibility:**

Life is full of surprises, and motherhood is no different. In Proverbs 19:21 (NIV), there's wisdom in recognising that countless are the plans in a person's heart, but it's the Lord's purpose that prevails. Cultivate adaptability and flexibility along your career.

- **Celebrate Milestones:**

In Ecclesiastes 3:1 (NIV), there's an awareness of the seasons of life: "There is a time for everything, and a season for every activity under the heavens." Celebrate the achievements, large and little, honouring the beauty of each season.

- **Navigating the Unknown:**

As you peek into the future, it's normal to experience a combination of exhilaration and anxiety. In Jeremiah 29:11 (NIV), there's a reassuring assurance: "For I know the plans I have for you, declares the Lord, plans to prosper you and not to harm you, plans to give you hope and a future." Embrace the uncertainty with the conviction that a higher plan is developing.

- **Embrace the Journey, Dad:**

So, my soon-to-be dad buddy, as you gaze forward into the huge expanse of parenting, remember that it's not about having all the answers or a failsafe guidebook. It's about relishing the trip, anticipating the pleasures and trials, and establishing a foundation of love and trust for the wonderful tapestry of moments that ahead. In Romans 15:13 (NIV), there's a blessing for hope and joy: "May the God of hope fill you with all joy and peace as you trust in him, so that you may overflow with hope by the power of the Holy Spirit." May your journey as a parent brim with hope, joy, and the solid confidence that you're not going alone. You've got this!

===

Reflections on the First Year

===

As you find yourself on the threshold of the wonderful trip called parenthood, let's take a time to discuss about something that may seem like a far shore right now — "Reflections on the First Year." I know, it could seem premature to discuss the first year when you're excitedly expecting the first cry and little fingers curling around yours. But believe me, this contemplation is not about racing forward; it's about creating a foundation for the wonderful, hard, and transforming days that lie ahead. So, have a seat, let's speak, and of course, I'll toss in some knowledge from the Good Book to illuminate your way.

The Uncharted Territory of Parenthood

As you stand on the edge of parenthood, the first year could feel like a foggy dream in the far future. Yet, in the blink of an eye, you'll find yourself thinking on a flurry of memories - the first grin, the restless nights, the modest successes, and the lessons learnt. It's an unfamiliar region filled with excitement, tiredness, and an abundance of love.

Why Reflect on the First Year: Before we dig into what the first year can offer, let's explore why reflection is a compass for the journey:

- **Celebrating Milestones:**

In Ecclesiastes 3:1-2 (NIV), there's an acknowledgment of the seasons of life: "There is a time for everything, and a season for every activity under the heavens: a time to be born and a time to die." The first year is a tapestry of milestones — the first laugh, the first tooth, the first steps. Reflection helps you to enjoy these times.

- **Learning and development:**

Just as your young one learns to crawl, walk, and explore, you, too, will experience significant development. In Proverbs 19:20 (NIV), there's wisdom in listening to advise: "Listen to advice and accept discipline, and at the end, you will be counted among the wise." Reflecting on your experiences enables you to learn and develop as a parent.

- **Navigating problems:**

The first year provides its share of problems, from restless nights to calming a screaming infant. In James 1:2-4 (NIV), there's understanding of the refining process of difficulties: "Consider it pure joy, my brothers and sisters, whenever you face trials of many kinds, because you know that the testing of your faith produces perseverance." Reflection allows you to handle obstacles with resilience and faith.

- **Building Family customs:**

Reflecting on the first year helps you create the framework for family customs. In Proverbs 22:6 (NIV), there's wisdom in bringing up a child: "Start children off on the way they should go, and even when they are old, they will not turn from it." Your purposeful activities in the first year build the traditions that persist.

What to Anticipate in the First Year:
Now, let's examine some insights of what the first year could contain for you:

- **Sleepless Nights and exhausted Smiles:**

Get ready for a rollercoaster of sleepless nights and exhausted smiles. In Psalm 121:3-4 (NIV), there's a reassuring assurance: "He will not let your foot slip—he who watches over you will not slumber; indeed, he who watches over Israel will neither slumber nor sleep." Even amid the fatigue, realise that you're not alone.

- **Unconditional Love:**

Anticipate an outpouring of unconditional love, both from you and towards you. In 1 Corinthians 16:14 (NIV), there's a command to do everything in love: "Do everything in love." Your love for your kid and their love for you build a deep tie.

- **Discovering New views:**

The first year is a voyage of discovering new views - from viewing the world through your baby's eyes to obtaining insights into your own heart. In Psalm 139:23-24 (NIV), there's a petition asking God to examine your heart: "examine me, God, and know my heart; test me and know my anxious thoughts. See whether there is any objectionable manner in me and guide me in the road eternal."

- **Parenting Instincts Kick In:**

Trust that your parenting instincts will kick in. In Proverbs 3:5-6 (NIV), there's wisdom in trusting the Lord with all your heart: "Trust in the Lord with all your heart and lean not on your own understanding; in all your ways submit to him, and he will make your paths straight." Trust the instincts that God has endowed you with.

How to Reflect on the First Year:

Now, let's speak about how to go about this reflection process, ensuring it becomes a vital compass for your journey:

- **Keep a Journal:**

In Habakkuk 2:2 (NIV), there's an exhortation to write down the revelation and make it clear: "Then the Lord replied: 'Write down the revelation and make it plain on tablets so that a herald may run with it.'" Keep a record of your thoughts, emotions, and the priceless moments.

- **Have Heart-to-Heart Conversations:**

In Proverbs 27:19 (NIV), there's an awareness that as water reflects the face, so one's life reflects the heart: "As water reflects the face, so one's life reflects the heart." Have heart-to-heart chats with your spouse, friends, or mentors about your experiences.

- **Enjoy accomplishments:**

Take time to enjoy the accomplishments, both great and little. In Philippians 4:13 (NIV), there's a reminder of God's power inside us: "I can do all this through him who gives me strength." Celebrate the strength you discover in situations of adversity.

- **Learn from Challenges:**

In Romans 5:3-4 (NIV), there's understanding of the character-building aspect of persistence: "Not only so, but we also glory in our sufferings, because we know that suffering produces perseverance; perseverance, character; and character, hope." Learn from the obstacles, understanding they develop your character and drive hope.

- **Navigating the Emotional Landscape:**

As you reminisce on the first year, be prepared for a panorama of emotions. In Psalm 34:18 (NIV), there's a consoling assurance: "The Lord is close to the brokenhearted and saves those who are crushed in spirit." It's acceptable to feel stressed, delighted, and everything in between. God is near in every feeling.

- **Embrace the Journey, Dad:**

As you ponder the first year of parenthood, remember that it's a journey, not a destination. Embrace the pleasures, learn from the struggles, and let love be your guiding light. In 1 Corinthians 13:4-7 (NIV), there's a wonderful depiction of love: "Love is patient, love is gentle. It does not envy, it does not brag, it is not boastful. It does not disrespect others, it is not self-seeking, it is not quickly angry, it maintains no record of wrongs. Love does not pleasure in wickedness but rejoices with the truth. It always defends, always trusts, always hopes, always perseveres." Let this love lead your thoughts, forming the beautiful story of the first year and setting the scene for the great chapters still to come. You've got this, dad!

Planning for the Future

As you stand on the threshold of parenthood, it's only natural for your thoughts to stretch beyond the immediate thrill of baby showers and nursery preparations. You could find yourself thinking what lies ahead, not just in the next few months but in the years to come. So, let's have a heart-to-heart on a subject that could seem a little hefty but is tremendously vital — "Planning for the Future."

The Horizon Beyond Diapers

I know, the near future is filled with diaper changes, restless nights, and the beautiful perfume of baby lotion. But believe me, it's never too early to cast your sight a little farther down the road. Planning for the future isn't just about financial investments or picking the appropriate school; it's about setting the scene for a life filled with purpose, love, and meaningful experiences.

Why Plan for the Future:
Before we dig into the practical issues, let's discuss why preparing for the future is a key component of your path into fatherhood:

- **Stewardship of Blessings:**

In Matthew 25:21 (NIV), there's an acknowledgment of diligent stewardship: "His lord said, 'Well done, good and loyal servant! You have been loyal with a few things; I will put you in control of many things. Come and share your master's delight!'" As a parent, you are entrusted with the great gift of a child, and preparing for the future is part of being a responsible steward.

- **Building a firm Foundation:**

In Luke 6:48 (NIV), there's wisdom in building on a firm foundation: "They are like a guy constructing a home, who dug down deep and built the foundation on rock. When a flood arrived, the stream hit the home but could not shake it, since it was firmly constructed." Planning for the future is about establishing a foundation that can endure life's storms.

- **Creating a Legacy:**

Proverbs 13:22 (NIV) alludes to the notion of leaving an inheritance: "A good person leaves an inheritance for their children's children, but a sinner's wealth is stored up for the righteous." Your goals for the future contribute to the legacy you leave for generations to come.

- **Providing Security:**

In 1 Timothy 5:8 (NIV), there's a charge to provide for one's home: "Anyone who does not provide for their relatives, and especially for their own household, has denied the faith and is worse than an unbeliever." Planning for the future is a means of creating security for your family.

What to Consider When preparing:

Now, let's break down some practical issues to consider as you begin on the adventure of preparing for the future:

Financial Preparation

Yes, this one may seem apparent, but it's worth addressing. In Proverbs 21:20 (NIV), there's wisdom in storing up choice food and olive oil: "The wise store up choice food and olive oil, but fools gulp theirs down." Begin by developing a budget, saving sensibly, and researching investments that correspond with your family's objectives.

- **Educational Goals:**

Proverbs 1:5 (NIV) highlights the significance of attaining wisdom: "Let the wise listen and add to their learning, and let the discerning get guidance." While your small one could be years away from school, establishing educational aspirations early on might help you make educated choices later.

- **Health and Well-being:**

In 1 Corinthians 6:19-20 (NIV), there's a reminder of our bodies being temples of the Holy Spirit: "Do you not know that your bodies are temples of the Holy Spirit, who is in you, whom you have received from God? You are not your own; you were purchased at a price. Therefore, worship God with your body." Planning for the future entails prioritizing health and well-being for both you and your family.

- **Spiritual Nurturing:**

As you prepare for the future, don't neglect the spiritual component. Proverbs 22:6 (NIV) advocates bringing up a kid in the way they should walk: "Start children off on the way they should go, and even when they are old, they will not turn from it." Consider how you'll encourage your child's spiritual development.

How to Start Planning:

Now, let's speak about practical measures you may take to start preparing for the future:

- **Define Your Values and Goals:**

In Proverbs 16:3 (NIV), there's wisdom in submitting your plans to the Lord: "Commit to the Lord whatever you do, and he will establish your plans." Start by identifying your beliefs and making clear objectives for your family. What matters most to you?

- **Create a Financial Plan:**

In Proverbs 24:27 (NIV), there's instruction in preparing your job outside and getting it ready for yourself: "Put your outdoor work in order and get your fields ready; after that, build your house." Begin with a sound financial strategy. This involves budgeting, saving, and contemplating long-term investments.

- **Investigate Educational possibilities:**

It's never too early to investigate educational possibilities. Proverbs 2:6 (NIV) alludes to the source of wisdom: "For the Lord gives wisdom; from his mouth come knowledge and understanding." Seek insight as you investigate educational pathways that match with your beliefs.

Prioritize Health and Well-being: In 1 Corinthians 10:31 (NIV), there's a command to do everything for the glory of God: "So whether you eat or drink or whatever you do, do it all for the glory of God." Prioritize the health and well-being of your family in all facets of life.

- **Navigating Uncertainty with Faith:**

As you continue on this road of preparing for the future, it's vital to understand that life is full with uncertainties. Proverbs 16:9 (NIV) tells us that we may plan our way, but the Lord determines our steps: "In their hearts humans plan their course, but the Lord establishes their steps." Navigating uncertainty with faith is a vital element of the process.

- **Embrace the Journey, Dad:**

In conclusion, my friend, preparing for the future is not about having every detail sorted out; it's about taking conscious efforts now that correspond with the vision you have for your family. As you negotiate this voyage into the future, know that you're not alone. In Jeremiah 29:11 (NIV), there's a reassuring assurance: "For I know the plans I have for you, declares the Lord, plans to prosper you and not to harm you, plans to give you hope and a future." Trust in the Lord's intentions, take active actions, and enjoy the path of preparing for a future filled with love, purpose, and the pleasure of raising a family. You've got this, dad!

Embracing Fatherhood Beyond Year One

As you travel the magnificent adventure of parenthood, there comes a time when you understand that it's not only about surviving the restless nights or mastering the hardships of the first year. It's about embracing parenting beyond that first flurry. So, let's have a conversation about "Embracing Fatherhood Beyond Year One."

The Evolution of Fatherhood

You've come a long way since those first hesitant diaper changes and restless nights, haven't you? The reality is, as your little one develops and experiences the world, your position as a parent alters too. Embracing fatherhood beyond the first year is about adjusting to the changing demands of your kid, developing your bond, and relishing the particular delights that each stage provides.

Why Embrace Fatherhood Beyond Year One:
Before we get into the practical issues, let's analyse why embracing fatherhood beyond the first year is an interesting and satisfying endeavor:

- **Building Lasting Connections:**

In Colossians 3:14 (NIV), there's a call to put on love, which binds everything together in perfect harmony: "And over all these virtues put on love, which binds them all together in perfect unity." Embracing fatherhood beyond the first year allows you to build lasting connections rooted in love.

- **Guiding and Nurturing:**

Proverbs 22:6 (NIV) refers to the value of early guidance: "Start children off on the way they should go, and even when they are old, they will not turn from it." Beyond the first year, you continue to lead and nurture your kid, helping mould their path.

- **Witnessing Milestones:**

The journey doesn't end after the first year; it unfolds with a succession of milestones — the first day of school, riding a bike, graduation. In Ecclesiastes 3:1 (NIV), there's an acknowledgment of the many seasons in life: "There is a time for everything, and a season for every activity under the heavens."

- **Modeling Character and Values:**

Beyond the early phases, you have the chance to model character and values. In Proverbs 20:7 (NIV), there's an acknowledgment of the virtuous who guide their children with integrity: "The righteous lead blameless lives; blessed are their children after them."

- **Navigating the Challenges:**

As you embrace parenthood beyond the first year, it's crucial to understand that each stage comes with its own set of obstacles. Proverbs 3:5-6 (NIV) teaches us to trust in the Lord: "Trust in the Lord with all your heart and lean not on your own understanding; in all your ways submit to him, and he will make your paths straight." Trusting in God's direction helps handle the problems with wisdom and grace.

What to Embrace Beyond Year One:

Now, let's discuss some characteristics to embrace as you continue your great journey:

- **Deeper talks:**

Beyond the first year, you'll find yourself involved in deeper talks with your kid. In Proverbs 4:7 (NIV), there's wisdom in gaining wisdom and knowledge: "The beginning of wisdom is this: Get wisdom. Though it cost all you have, get understanding."

- **Shared Hobbies and Interests:**

As your kid develops, you may share hobbies and interests. In Ecclesiastes 4:9-10 (NIV), there's appreciation of the strength in companionship: "Two are better than one because they have a good return for their labor: If either of them falls down, one can help the other up."

- **Supporting personality:**

Beyond the first year, you'll watch the flowering of your child's personality. In Psalm 139:14 (NIV), there's a magnificent recognition of being fearfully and wonderfully formed: "I praise you because I am fearfully and wonderfully made; your works are wonderful, I know that full well."

- **Encouraging Independence:**

Proverbs 16:9 (NIV) speaks to the human heart planning its course but the Lord establishing the steps: "In their hearts humans plan their course, but the Lord establishes their steps." Embrace the journey of encouraging your child's independence, knowing that God guides their steps.

How to Embrace Fatherhood Beyond Year One:

Now, let's speak about practical measures you may do to truly enjoy parenthood beyond the first stages:

- **Quality Time:**

In Psalm 90:12 (NIV), there's an awareness of the worth of time: "Teach us to number our days, that we may gain a heart of wisdom." Spend quality time with your kid, making memories that endure a lifetime.

- **Active Listening:**

James 1:19 (NIV) advises us to be quick to listen and slow to talk: "My dear brothers and sisters, take note of this:

Everyone should be quick to listen, slow to speak and slow to become angry." Practice active listening while your kid discusses their ideas and emotions.

- **Encouragement and Affirmation:**

In Ephesians 4:29 (NIV), there's a call to speak only what is helpful for building others up: "Do not let any unwholesome talk come out of your mouths, but only what is helpful for building others up according to their needs, that it may benefit those who listen." Encourage and affirm your child's efforts and achievements.

- **Prayer and direction:**

Proverbs 3:6 (NIV) urges us to recognise the Lord in all our ways: "in all your ways submit to him, and he will make your paths straight." Seek direction via prayer as you negotiate the complexity of parenthood.

- **Facing the Future with Hope:**

As you accept parenthood beyond the first year, confront the future with optimism. In Jeremiah 29:11 (NIV), there's a reassuring assurance: "For I know the plans I have for you, declares the Lord, plans to prosper you and not to harm you, plans to give you hope and a future." Trust in the plans God has for you and your kid.

- **Embrace the Journey, Dad:**

In conclusion, my buddy, as you continue to embrace parenthood, remember that it's an ever-evolving process. Enjoy the current times, relish the distinct delights of each stage, and approach the future with hope and confidence in the Lord. In Isaiah 41:10 (NIV), there's a promise of God's presence and aid: "So do not fear, for I am with you; do not be dismayed, for I am your God. I will strengthen you and help you; I will uphold you with my righteous right hand." Embrace the trip, dad - the best is yet to come!

==

Lessons Learned

==

As you embark on this remarkable journey called fatherhood, let's take a moment to reflect on something that's an integral part of the adventure – "Lessons Learned." Oh yes, there's a whole lot to discover and absorb on this path of parenting, and each lesson is like a nugget of wisdom that shapes you into the dad you're destined to be.

The Classroom of Fatherhood

Imagine parenting as a large and vibrant school, where every day is a lesson, and each event is a teacher. From the earliest moments of holding your infant in your arms to navigating the adolescent years, the classroom of fatherhood is replete with lessons that not only shape your kid but sculpt you into a wiser and more compassionate parent.

Why Embrace Lessons Learned:
Before we get into the practical components, let's analyse why accepting lessons learnt is a critical facet of your path into fatherhood:

- **Growth Through Challenges:**

In James 1:2-4 (NIV), there's a recognition of the refining process through trials: "Consider it pure joy, my brothers and sisters, whenever you face trials of many kinds because you know that the testing of your faith produces perseverance. Let perseverance finish its work so that you may be mature and complete, not lacking anything." Lessons learned often come through challenges, and they contribute to your growth as a dad.

- **Building Resilience:**

Proverbs 24:16 (NIV) speaks to the resilience that comes from falling and getting up again: "for though the righteous fall seven times, they rise again, but the wicked stumble when calamity strikes." Fatherhood is a journey of resilience, and each lesson learned strengthens your ability to rise after a stumble.

- **Deepening Understanding:**

Proverbs 4:7 (NIV) highlights the significance of learning: "The beginning of wisdom is this: Get wisdom. Though it cost all you have, get understanding." Lessons learnt enhance your understanding of your kid, yourself, and the complicated dance of motherhood.

- **Shaping Character:**

Proverbs 22:6 (NIV) underscores the impact of early training: "Start children off on the way they should go, and even when they are old, they will not turn from it." Lessons learned in the early stages of fatherhood contribute to shaping your character and the character of your child.

What Lessons Fatherhood Teaches:

Now, let's review some of the vital skills that parenthood is sure to offer you:

- Patience: Oh, the virtue of patience! Fatherhood teaches you that sometimes the finest things in life take time. In Ecclesiastes 7:8 (NIV), there's an awareness that patience is better than pride: "The end of a matter is better than its beginning, and patience is better than pride."

- Unconditional Love: 1 Corinthians 13:4-7 (NIV) beautifully describes love: "Love is patient, love is kind. It does not envy, it does not boast, it is not proud. It does not dishonor others, it is not self-seeking, it is not easily angered, it keeps no record of wrongs. Love does not delight in evil but rejoices with the truth. It always protects, always trusts, always hopes, always perseveres." Fatherhood unveils the depth of unconditional love.

- Flexibility: In a world that's always changing, parenting teaches you the skill of flexibility. Proverbs 2:6 (NIV) points to the source of wisdom: "For the Lord gives wisdom; from his mouth come knowledge and understanding." Wisdom from above aids you in adjusting to the ever-evolving needs of your kid.

- Humility: Fatherhood is a humbling process. Proverbs 16:18 (NIV) admits the danger of pride: "Pride goes before destruction, a haughty spirit before a fall." Lessons learnt frequently occur in times of humility, reminding you that you don't have all the answers, and that's good.

How to Embrace Lessons Learned:

Now, let's speak about how to actively accept the teachings that parenthood offers:

- **Reflect Regularly:**

In Psalm 119:105 (NIV), there's a recognition of God's word as a lamp to our feet and a light to our route: "Your word is a lamp for my feet, a light on my path." Regular contemplation, possibly via writing, helps you to see the lessons lighted on your journey.

- **Seek Guidance:**

Proverbs 3:5-6 (NIV) encourages us to trust in the Lord and lean not on our understanding: "Trust in the Lord with all your heart and lean not on your own understanding; in all your ways submit to him, and he will make your paths straight." Seek guidance in prayer and through the wisdom of trusted mentors or fellow dads.

- **Celebrate Progress:**

In Philippians 1:6 (NIV), there's assurance that God will carry to completion the good work He began in you: "being confident of this, that he who began a good work in you will carry it on to completion until the day of Christ Jesus." Celebrate the progress you make in applying lessons learned.

- **Extend Grace:**

James 4:6 (NIV) reminds us that God provides grace to the humble: "But he gives us more grace. That is why Scripture says: 'God opposes the proud but shows favor to the humble.'" Extend grace to yourself and others as you negotiate the learning curve of parenthood.

Navigating Mistakes with Grace:

It's crucial to know that errors are unavoidable on this road. Proverbs 24:16 (NIV) alludes about the virtuous falling but rising again: "for though the righteous fall seven times, they rise again." Navigating errors with grace, learning from them, and going ahead is a crucial element of accepting lessons learned.

- **Embrace the Journey, Dad:**

In closing, my friend, as you embrace the teachings that parenthood provides, remember that each mistake is an opportunity to rise stronger, each obstacle is a chance to become wiser, and each lesson acquired creates the beautiful story of your path. In Philippians 4:13 (NIV), there's a reminder of the strength inside you: "I can do all this through him who gives me strength." Embrace the journey, dad, with an open heart and a teachable spirit. You've got this!

CONCLUSION

As we close our trip through "Daily Devotions for New Dads," I want to express my deepest congratulations to each one of you. You've begun on an astonishing voyage, navigating the peaks and valleys of parenthood with love, bravery, and a dedication to progress.

Reflections on the Journey:
As you ponder on the pages of this book, I hope you've discovered inspiration, insight, and a feeling of companionship. Fatherhood is not a lonesome journey but a shared excursion with countless fathers throughout the globe, each confronting unique problems and cherishing own victories.

An Ongoing Conversation:
This book is not the conclusion of the debate; rather, it's a continuation of the discourse about the great privilege and responsibility of being a dad. The chapters have looked into many dimensions of parenting - from the wonderful moments of playfulness with your infant to the weightier aspects of managing problems and dealing with stress.

An Ever-Evolving Journey:
Fatherhood is an ever-evolving adventure, much like the seasons that change, bringing new experiences and lessons. Proverbs 3:5-6 (NIV) advises us to trust in the Lord with all our hearts and rely not on our understanding. Trust in the Lord, fathers, as you navigate the unknowns and uncertainties of the future.

A Tapestry of Love:
Through establishing routines, supporting your spouse, and creating family rituals, you've been weaving a tapestry of love within your house. This tapestry is not only a collection of experiences but a legacy that resonates through the generations. Your dedication to creating solid bonds and embracing fatherhood beyond the first year is impacting not just your child's future but the future of your family.

A Letter to Your Future Self:
In the spirit of "A Letter to Your Future Self," visualise the parent you wish to be. See the moments of laughing, the shared successes, and the profound ties with your kid. Proverbs 16:9 (NIV) reassures us that, while we may plan our way, the Lord determines our steps. Embrace each step with purpose and a heart open to the teachings that come your way.

Lessons Learned:
Reflect on the lessons learnt — the patience nurtured, the unconditional love found, and the resilience that has become a part of your dad arsenal. Proverbs 24:16 (NIV) accepts that the upright may fall seven times, but they rise again. It's in the rising, in the learning from errors, that progress occurs.

Facing the Future with Hope:
As you plan for the future, remember Jeremiah 29:11 (NIV): "For I know the plans I have for you, declares the Lord, plans to prosper you and not to harm you, plans to give you hope and a future." Face the future with hope, trusting that God's plans for you and your family are filled with goodness and purpose.

Embracing Fatherhood Beyond Year One:
The notion of "Embracing Fatherhood Beyond Year One" is a poignant reminder that your job as a parent is a dynamic and continuing adventure. Isaiah 40:31 (NIV) informs us that people who trust in the Lord will replenish their strength. As you accept the various phases of parenthood, find refreshment and strength in the optimism that accompanies the promise of each new day.

A Call to Celebrate:
Celebrate the milestones, large and little, because they signify the passage of time and progress. In Ecclesiastes 3:1 (NIV), we are reminded that there is a season for everything.

Your job as a parent grows, and each stage offers its own set of delights and difficulties. Embrace them with a heart full of appreciation.

A Final Word:
In this last chapter, may these words serve as a final exhortation: Embrace the adventure, fathers. Embrace the uncertainty, the joys, the struggles, and the successes. Embrace the responsibility with love, because love is the foundation upon which the legacy of your family is created.

May your days be filled with the warmth of your child's joy, the knowledge to handle hurdles, and the grace to cherish the wonderful moments. Thank you for taking this journey with "Daily Devotions for New Dads." May your fatherhood narrative be one of everlasting love, unbreakable strength, and unbounded joy.

With kind regards

Made in the USA
Columbia, SC
31 July 2025